5.99

WORKBOOK
REVISE
AQA GCSE
ENGLISH
LANGUAGE

TARGETING GRADE 5

efore the date below

Esther Menon
CONSULTANT: HELEN BACKHOUSE

OXFORD

UNIVERSITY PRESS

OXFORD
UNIVERSITY PRESS

Great Clarendon Street, Oxford, OX2 6DP, United Kingdom

Oxford University Press is a department of the University of Oxford.

It furthers the University's objective of excellence in research, scholarship, and education by publishing worldwide. Oxford is a registered trade mark of Oxford University Press in the UK and in certain other countries

© Oxford University Press 2016

First published in 2016

British Library Cataloguing in Publication Data

Data available

ISBN 978-019-835919-7

10 9 8 7 6 5

Printed in India by Multivista Global Pvt. Ltd

Acknowledgements

The author and publisher are grateful for permission to reprint extracts from the following copyright material:

Beryl Bainbridge: *Every Man for Himself* (Abacus, 2002), copyright © Beryl Bainbridge 1996, reprinted by permission of the4 Little, Brown Book Group Ltd.

Charlie Brooker: 'Apple's software updates are like changing water in a fish tank: I'd rather let the fish die', *The Guardian*, 22 Sept 2014, copyright © Guardian News & Media Ltd 2014, reprinted by permission of GNM Ltd.

Christy Brown: *My Left Foot* (Secker & Warburg 1954), reprinted by permission of the Random House Group Ltd.

Jack Cope: 'Power' from *Selected Stories by Jack Cope* (Africa South, 1986), reprinted by permission of New Africa Books (Pty) Ltd.

Daphne du Maurier: *The Birds* (Penguin, 1952), copyright © The Chichester Partnership 1952, reprinted by permission of Curtis Brown Group Ltd, London on behalf of Chichester Partnership

Nicci French: *Until It's Over* (Michael Joseph, 2007), copyright © Nicci French 2009, reprinted by permission of Penguin Books Ltd.

Stephen Fry: *Moab my Washpot* (Arrow, 2004/ Hutchinson 1997), copyright © Stephen Fry 1997, reprinted by permission of David Higham Associates.

Rose George: 'The hunter who killed Cecil the lion doesn't deserve our empathy', *The Guardian*, 29 July 2015, copyright © Guardian News & Media Ltd 2015, reprinted by permission of GNM Ltd.

Suzanne Goldenberg: 'Shark Attack survivors fight to save endangered species', *The Guardian*, 19 Sept 2010, copyright © Guardian News & Media Ltd 2010, reprinted by permission of GNM Ltd.

Anthony Horowitz: *The House of Silk* (Orion, 2011), copyright © Anthony Horowitz 2011, reprinted by permission of The Orion Publishing Group.

Tim Lott: *Under the Same Stars* (Simon & Schuster, 2012), copyright © Tim Lott 2012, reprinted by permission of Simon & Schuster.

Michelle Paver: *Dark Matter* (Orion, 2010), copyright © Michelle Paver 2010, reprinted by permission of The Orion Publishing Group.

Kira Salak: *The Cruelest Journey: 600 Miles to Timbuktu* (National Geographic Books, 2004), reprinted by permission of The National Geographic Society.

Chris Smith: 'Dress to Impress: what to wear to a job interview', *The Guardian*, 15 July 2014, copyright © Guardian News & Media Ltd 2014, reprinted by permission of GNM Ltd.

Fay Weldon: 'A Letter to my Sixteen Year-Old Self', copyright © Fay Weldon 2009, from *Dear Me: A Letter to My Sixteen Year-old Self* (Simon & Schuster, 2009), reprinted by permission of Fay Weldon c/o Georgina Capel Associates, 29 Wardour Street, London W1D 6PS.

Jeanette Winterson: *Tanglewreck* (Bloomsbury Children's Books, 2006), copyright © Jeanette Winterson 2006, reprinted by permission of Bloomsbury Publishing Plc.

John Wyndham: *The Midwich Cuckoos* (Michael Joseph, 1957), reprinted by permission of David Higham Associates.

The author and publisher would like to thank the following for permission to use their photographs:

Cover: Christian Musat / Shutterstock

p58: Terry Mathews / Alamy Stock Photo; **p68**: design36 / Shutterstock; **p76**: Maksim Shmeljov / Shutterstock; **p79**: Glynnis Jones / Shutterstock; **p155**: Andrey Yurlov / Shutterstock;

Artwork by Q2A Media

Although we have made every effort to trace and contact all copyright holders before publication this has not been possible in all cases. If notified, the publisher will rectify any errors or omissions at the earliest opportunity.

Contents

AQA GCSE English Language specification overview

The exam papers

The grade you receive at the end of your AQA GCSE English Language course is entirely based on your performance in two exam papers. The following provides a summary of these two exam papers:

Exam paper	Reading and Writing questions and marks	Assessment Objectives	Timing	Marks (and % of GCSE)
Paper 1: Explorations in creative reading and writing	Section A: Reading Exam text: • One unseen literature fiction text Exam questions and marks: • One short form question (1 x 4 marks) • Two longer form questions (2 x 8 marks) • One extended question (1 x 20 marks)	Reading: • AO1 • AO2 • AO4	1 hour 45 minutes	Reading: 40 marks (25% of GCSE) Writing: 40 marks (25% of GCSE) Paper 1 total: 80 marks (50% of GCSE)
	Section B: Writing Descriptive or narrative writing Exam question and marks: • One extended writing question (24 marks for content, 16 marks for technical accuracy)	Writing: • AO5 • AO6		
Paper 2: Writers' viewpoints and perspectives	Section A: Reading Exam text: • One unseen non-fiction text and one unseen literary non-fiction text Exam questions and marks: • One short form question (1 x 4 marks) • Two longer form questions (1 x 8 marks and 1 x 12 marks) • One extended question (1 x 16 marks)	Reading: • AO1 • AO2 • AO3	1 hour 45 minutes	Reading: 40 marks (25% of GCSE) Writing: 40 marks (25% of GCSE) Paper 2 total: 80 marks (50% of GCSE)
	Section B: Writing Writing to present a viewpoint Exam question and marks: • One extended writing question (24 marks for content, 16 marks for technical accuracy)	Writing: • AO5 • AO6		

How this workbook is structured

Self-evaluations

In order to get the most out of your revision, we would recommend firstly completing the Reading and Writing self-evaluation checklists on pages 6 to 9. These checklists will help you identify strengths and weaknesses so that you, and your teacher, can ensure that your revision is focused and targeted.

Reading

The Reading sections of this workbook take you through the requirements of each question in the two exam papers. As well as guidance and activities, you will also find extracts of sample student responses, marked with commentaries. There are spaces to write your answers into throughout the workbook.

Writing

The Writing sections of this workbook focus on preparing you for the types of writing you will face in the two exam papers. You will also find a range of strategies to help you when approaching the writing tasks as well as practice opportunities.

Sample exam papers

The workbook concludes with two full sample exam papers, one for Paper 1 and one for Paper 2.

What are the main features within this workbook?

Activities and texts

To help you practise your reading responses, you will find activities throughout this workbook are all linked to the types of questions you will face in your exams. The source texts also reflect the types of texts you will be reading and responding to in your exams.

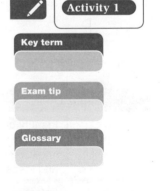

Exam tips, Key terms and glossed words

These features help support your understanding of key terms, concepts and more difficult words within a source text. These therefore enable you to concentrate fully on developing your exam response skills.

Progress check

You will find regular formative assessments in the form of 'Progress checks'. These enable you to establish how confident you feel about what you have been learning and help you to identify areas for further practice.

 **Progress check**

Reading skills self-evaluation

Assessing your skills

Before you start your GCSE English Language revision you need to know which skills you need to focus on. When you revise you should spend the maximum amount of time on skills you feel less confident about.

Use the table below to evaluate your reading skills.

First, look back over your work, including any reading tests you have done. Note the types of questions you did well and the ones that you found more difficult.

Then, for each skill identified in the table, decide whether your work shows you reaching the target Grade 5 skills descriptors or if you are still working at the basic skills level. You should only tick one box in each row.

Paper and question	Skill	Basic skills descriptors	Check ✔	Target Grade 5 skills descriptor	Check ✔
Reading Paper 1 only					
Question 1	Identify explicit information and ideas	I can identify some explicit information and ideas.		I can accurately identify four explicit ideas or pieces of information.	
Question 3	Analyse how writers use structure to achieve effects	I am aware of structure and can make a simple comment on its effect.		I can show **clear** understanding when I **explain clearly** the effects of a writer's choice of structural features.	
Question 4	Evaluate texts critically	I can show limited understanding of a writer's methods and offer a simple, **limited** evaluative comment on the text.		I can **critically** evaluate the text in a **clear** and **relevant** way.	
Reading Paper 2 only					
Question 1	Identify and interpret explicit and implicit information and ideas	I can identify some explicit information and ideas.		I can identify and interpret explicit and implicit information and ideas.	
Question 2	Select and synthesize evidence from two texts	I can show a simple awareness from one or both texts, offering paraphrase rather than inference, making simple reference to evidence from one or both texts and making statements to show simple differences between texts.		I can show clear synthesis and interpretation of both texts by making clear inferences, selecting clear and relevant references and textual detail, and making statements that show clear differences between the texts	

Paper and question	Skills	Basic skills descriptors	Check ✔	Target Grade 5 skills descriptors	Check ✔
Reading Paper 2 only continued					
Question 4	Compare how writers convey their ideas and perspectives across two texts	I can show a simple awareness of ideas and/or perspectives, identifying writers' methods in a simple way and make simple references.		I can make **clear** and **relevant** comparisons between texts, showing clear understanding of different ideas and perspectives, and **explain clearly** how writers' methods are used, selecting relevant detail to support.	
Reading Paper 1 and Paper 2					
Paper 1 Question 2 and Paper 2 Question 3	Use relevant subject terminology	I can make simple and mainly appropriate use of subject terminology when writing about language and structure.		I can make **clear** and **accurate** use of subject terminology when writing about language and structure.	
Paper 1 Question 2 and Paper 2 Question 3	Analyse how writers use language to achieve effects	I can make simple comments on the effects of language.		I can show **clear** understanding when I **explain clearly** the effects of the writer's choices of language.	
All reading questions except Paper 1 Question 1 and Paper 2 Question 1	Support your ideas with textual references	I can select simple references or textual details.		I can select and use a **range** of **relevant** textual details.	

 # My target skills

Look back at your completed self-evaluation table. You could check this with your teacher to see if they agree. Now list five skills you need to improve to reach the target Grade 5 skills descriptors.

1 ---

2 ---

3 ---

4 ---

5 ---

Writing skills self-evaluation

Assessing your skills

Now evaluate your writing skills in a similar way, using the table below.

First, look back over any writing tasks you have done. These should include narrative and descriptive writing tasks and writing to present a viewpoint. Note the types of tasks you did well and the ones that you found more difficult. Remember to use your teacher's comments to help you.

Then, for each skill listed in the table, decide whether your work reaches the target Grade 5 skills descriptors or if you are still working at the basic skills level. You should only tick one box in each row.

Basic skills descriptors	Check ✔	Target Grade 5 skills descriptor	Check ✔
I can show simple awareness of register and audience in my writing.		I can consistently match the register I use in my writing to the audience I am writing for.	
I show simple awareness of the need to match my writing to purpose.		My writing is consistently matched to purpose.	
I use simple vocabulary and simple linguistic devices in my writing.		I can choose vocabulary for effect and use a range of linguistic devices to achieve effects.	
I use some relevant ideas in my writing and simply link these.		My writing is engaging with a range of connected ideas.	
I try to use paragraphs, but my paragraphing is sometimes random.		I can use clear paragraphs and link them using discourse markers, although sometimes my paragraphing could be clearer.	
I can use some simple structural features in my writing.		I can usually use a variety of structural features effectively.	
I usually write in full sentences and can use full stops and capital letters accurately.		I can usually write in full and accurate sentences.	
I can use some punctuation marks, for example, question marks and speech marks.		I can usually use a range of punctuation.	
I try to use different sentence forms in my writing.		I can use a variety of sentence forms in my writing to achieve specific effects on the reader.	
I can use some Standard English and grammar, for example, verbs agree with their subject, and maintain the tense of a written piece.		I can usually control my use of Standard English and grammar.	
I can spell basic words and some more complex words accurately.		I can generally spell correctly, including complex and irregular words.	
I can use a variety of vocabulary, including some complex words.		I can use a range of vocabulary, including some sophisticated words.	

My target skills

Look back at your completed self-evaluation table. Check your teacher agrees with your evaluations. Now tick five skills from the list below that you think are the most important for you to improve in order to reach your target grade.

☐ Communicating clearly

☐ Writing in the appropriate style, register and tone for the task set

☐ Choosing vocabulary and linguistic devices to affect the reader

☐ Using and connecting together interesting ideas

☐ Using paragraphs and language that links them together

☐ Using structural features effectively

☐ Writing in full and accurate sentences

☐ Using a range of punctuation

☐ Using a range of different sentence lengths and forms to achieve specific effects

☐ Using Standard English appropriately

☐ Spelling accurately

☐ Using a range of vocabulary including some sophisticated words

Remember to target these skills as you complete the writing sections in this workbook.

Paper 1: Explorations in creative reading and writing

Overview of the exam paper

This exam lasts 1 hour 45 minutes and the exam paper is split into two sections.

Section A: Reading

- In this section you will read *one fiction text* from the 20th or 21st century and show your understanding of how the writer uses narrative and descriptive techniques to capture the interest of the reader.

- You will have to answer four questions.

- This section is worth 40 marks.

Section B: Writing

- In this section you will write your own creative text, linked to the theme that appears in the reading section. You will show your descriptive or narrative skills in response to a written prompt or picture.

- This section is worth 40 marks.

How your reading will be marked

Below is a table to remind you of the Assessment Objectives (AOs) that you will be tested on in the Reading section of Paper 1.

Assessment Objective	The reading skills that you need to demonstrate
AO1	Identify and interpret explicit and implicit information and ideas.
AO2	Explain, comment on and analyse how writers use language and structure to achieve effects and influence readers, using relevant subject terminology to support views.
AO4	Evaluate texts critically and support this with appropriate textual references.

In this chapter, you will practise these skills and learn exactly how and where to demonstrate them in the Paper 1 exam in order to achieve your target grade.

How your writing will be marked

Your writing will be marked against two Assessment Objectives.

Assessment Objective	The writing skills that you need to demonstrate
AO5 (Content and organization)	Communicate clearly, effectively and imaginatively, selecting and adapting tone, style and register for different forms, purposes and audiences. Organize information and ideas, using structural and grammatical features to support coherence and cohesion of texts.
AO6 (Technical accuracy)	Use a range of vocabulary and sentence structures for clarity, purpose and effect, with accurate spelling and punctuation.

The writing question in Paper 1 is worth a maximum of 40 marks:

- 24 marks are available for content and organization (AO5)
- 16 marks are available for technical accuracy (AO6).

What is content and organization?

To gain good marks for content and organization you need to:

- get your ideas across to the reader clearly
- match your writing to the purpose, audience and form you have been given.

You will need to make deliberate choices of language and textual features, so that your writing has the intended impact on readers. To assess this, the examiner will look at:

- the way you use individual words and phrases
- the way you sequence, link and present your ideas
- the organization of your piece of writing as a whole, and of the paragraphs and sections within it.

What is technical accuracy?

Technical accuracy is using words, punctuation and grammar correctly. Your written response needs to show that you can:

- use a range of vocabulary
- spell correctly, including more complex and sophisticated words
- write in correctly punctuated sentences
- use a variety of sentence forms to achieve specific effects
- write in Standard English.

Question 1

Identifying explicit information and ideas

This question assesses your ability to find **explicit** information in a specific section of the source text.

In the exam you should follow these steps to help you answer the question:

0 minutes

Step 1 Underline key terms in the question
To make sure you are answering the question that has been asked.

Step 2 Mark up the section of the text that you have been asked to select from. Draw a box around it.
It is no good finding answers in the wider extract if you have been asked to select from a small section.

Step 3 Underline key words and phrases in the source text that link to the question.
That way you know you are answering the question asked.

Step 4 Write your list in answer to the question. Remember to only write down answers that are found in the specific section of the source text.
You can **paraphrase** *evidence from the text, using your own words to identify the different pieces of relevant information.*

8 minutes

Activity 1

Read lines 11 to 20 of the source text on the opposite page. List four things we learn about Carson's father that morning.

A. ....

B. ....

C. ....

D. ....

In this extract, Carson Nash remembers his childhood and how he tried to get his father's attention by making Airfix kits (model aircraft assembled from different parts, glued together and painted).

Under the Same Stars by Tim Lott

Carson had saved for the Airfix kit of the **Focke-Wulf FW189 'Flying Eye' reconnaissance** plane with his own pocket money and it had taken him an entire week's worth of spare time to assemble it. The final result had justified the effort. The glued
5   seams showed no trace of **seepage**. It had taken painstaking application of eleven kinds of paint to complete the **livery** on the unique twin-boom design. The MG 15 machine gun in the rear cone looked excitingly poised for action. The **transfers** had taken perfectly – blue, white and red German crosses on the wings and
10   tailfin, with yellow 'Eastern Front' markings on the wing tips.

On the morning of his father's birthday, he had presented it to Dad, just before he left for work, as he was hurriedly finishing his breakfast of Rice Crispies and marmalade toast. His father had taken the unwrapped gift from Carson's small, eager hands, which
15   were still sticky with glue, and he had smiled and said thank you politely. He examined the model plane for a moment, from several angles.

Very nice, he had said. *Very nice*.

Then he put the plane on the kitchen windowsill, checked his
20   watch and left for work.

When it remained there, unclaimed and unremarked upon by his father for a further week, Carson took it to his room and with a small hammer that he had taken from his father's toolkit, smashed it to pieces and threw it in the dustbin. His father never said
25   anything about the disappearance of the gift.

Glossary

Focke-Wulf FW189 'Flying Eye': a German fighter plane used in the Second World War

reconnaissance: inspection of an area, especially by the military

seepage: leaking

livery: the paint scheme on an aircraft

transfers: designs that are moved from a sheet of paper to an object, similar to stickers

Activity 2

Now look at a student's answers to the question in Activity 1 below. Mark the answers as correct or incorrect with a tick or a cross. Explain the error in any that you have marked as incorrect using the sentence starter: 'This is incorrect because...'. One answer has been done for you.

A. Carson's father was rushing to get to work. _____

_____

B. Carson's father tried to balance the needs of his son with his need to get to work. _____

_____

C. He didn't wrap the present. _X_ This is incorrect because it describes Carson's actions_

rather than what we learn about his father. _____

D. He didn't notice that the model disappeared from where he left it. _____

_____

Progress check

Look back at your answer to Activity 1 on page 12. Use the following checklist to assess each point in your list.

	Yes	No
Is it true?		
Is it from the right section of text?		
Does it answer what the question asked?		

If you have answered no to any of these questions, change your answer for this point.

Using language to achieve effects

This question assesses your ability to explain the effects of a writer's choices of language. To produce a Grade 5 response you must:

- show *clear understanding* when you explain the effects of the writer's choices of language

- select and use a *range* of *relevant* textual detail (i.e. quotations and examples)

- use subject terminology *clearly* and *accurately*.

The words in italics above indicate what will distinguish a Grade 5 response from a weaker answer. You will explore exactly how to demonstrate each of these skills when answering Question 2 as you work through this section.

Activity 1

1. Look again at what you must do to achieve a Grade 5 response to Question 2. Choose the top four elements from the list below that *must* be included in a Grade 5 answer.

   ☐ Relevant textual detail (i.e. quotations and examples)

   ☐ Explanation of the writer's choice of language

   ☐ Comments about the audience of the text

   ☐ One quotation to support your answer

   ☐ Comments about the writer's life

   ☐ Language terminology, for example, noun, metaphor, short sentences

   ☐ Explanation of the effects of the language used

   ☐ Comments on the text's structure

   ☐ Comments about whether you like or dislike the text

Exam tip

You should spend 15 minutes reading the text and questions in Paper 1. Allow one minute per mark on each question in the Reading section to write your answer, for example for Question 2 worth 8 marks, spend 8 minutes, plus checking time.

Answering the question

Question 2 will present you with a short extract taken from the source text you have read. Look at the following example Question 2 which includes an extract from *Dark Matter* by Michelle Paver, which was published in 2010. This extract is set in the Arctic and describes a young man exploring the landscape alone.

Dark Matter by Michelle Paver

As I climbed higher, the going got tougher. I found myself stumbling over naked **scree** and brittle black **lichen**. The wind was sharp, and I was soon chilled. Clouds obscured the icecap, but I felt its freezing breath. When I took off my hat, my skull began to ache within seconds.

5 Behind the hiss of the wind and the chatter of the stream, the land lay silent. I passed the skeleton of a reindeer. I came to a standing stone by a small, cold lake. I stopped. I was aware of the noises around me – the wind, the water, my panting breath – but somehow they only deepened the stillness. I felt it as a physical presence. Immense.

10 Overwhelming. I realised that this place is, and will always be, no-man's-land.

Glossary

scree: small loose stones
lichen: a type of plant that grows on rocks

Example Exam Question

2 Look in detail at the extract from the source.

How does the writer use language to describe the impact of the Arctic setting?

You could include the writer's choice of:

- words and phrases
- language features and techniques
- sentence forms

In the exam, you should follow the steps below to help you to answer this question.

Step 1 Read the question and identify the key effect the question is asking you to analyse, that is, 'the impact of the Arctic setting'.

Step 2 Now read the extract again and underline sections that show:
- words and phrases chosen for effect
- language features, for example, metaphors
- sentence forms and patterns, for example, complex sentences.

Step 3 Write your answer to the question.
Remember to include the details you've underlined in the extract.

Step 4 Check your answer.

Establishing clear understanding

Remember, before you can begin to answer Question 2, you need to make sure you understand:

● the question

  and

● the extract.

Activity 2

Re-read the example Question 2 on page 16.

1. Underline or circle the words that tell you the focus of the language you must identify.

2. Write your own definitions for the following words and phrases from the extract. Remember to check the glossary terms to see if any of these words are explained. If not, work out their meaning from the text that surrounds them.

   obscured _____

   immense _____

   no-man's land _____

3. Circle the two words below that you think best describe the overall effect of the writer's description of the Arctic setting.

   hostile   dangerous   invigorating   isolated   spooky   cold

Explaining the effects of language

To explain the effects of language you must understand:

● what is being described and the overall effect the writer is trying to convey

● particular choices the writer has made

● why the language used works well to convey the situation, character or setting

● the effect on the reader.

In Activity 2, you identified the effect of the writer's description of the Arctic setting. To answer Question 2, link the effect to the language features used. Then, explain how these features work within the text.

Take a look at another example Question 2.

Example Exam Question

2 How does the writer use language to describe the narrator's life in the Arctic?

Now look at the following sentences which are taken from a different extract from *Dark Matter* by Michelle Paver. Here, the narrator is lifting his husky dog to treat an injury. To answer the question, a student has annotated this sentence with some initial notes about the overall effect the writer is trying to convey and the language features used to achieve this.

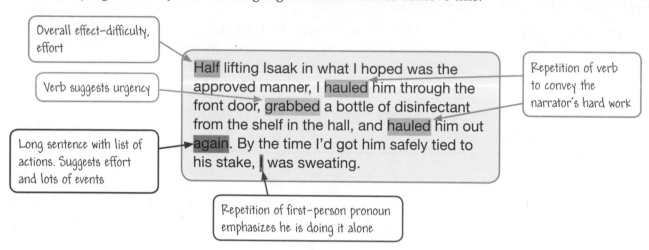

Overall effect–difficulty, effort

Verb suggests urgency

Long sentence with list of actions. Suggests effort and lots of events

Half lifting Isaak in what I hoped was the approved manner, I hauled him through the front door, grabbed a bottle of disinfectant from the shelf in the hall, and hauled him out again. By the time I'd got him safely tied to his stake, I was sweating.

Repetition of verb to convey the narrator's hard work

Repetition of first-person pronoun emphasizes he is doing it alone

Look at these extracts from two students' answers to the above exam question.

Student A

The writer shows that life in the Arctic is difficult. The writer describes the narrator lifting his dog. The writer's choice of language reflects the narrator's difficulties. The long complex sentence shows that it was a long process. The word 'grabbed' suggests the narrator is worried and rushing to snatch the bottle. The verb 'hauled' suggests the job of lifting the dog is hard. The repetition of this word underlines how difficult it is. It creates alliteration which sounds like the man is out of breath. This makes the reader admire the man and understand how tough his life is.

Student B

The writer says 'I hauled him through the front door, grabbed a bottle of disinfectant from the shelf in the hall, and hauled him out again'. The phrase 'hauled him out again' emphasizes that it was hard work. It shows that he is having a tough life. The dog is very heavy which is why he uses the word 'hauled' again as it shows he is heavy.

Activity 3

1. Annotate Student A's and Student B's answers by placing a number where you find evidence of the following key features of a Grade 5 response.

   1 Identifies the overall effect the writer is trying to achieve through their use of language.

   2 Selects relevant examples of language from the text.

   3 Clearly explains how the examples achieve the effect on the reader.

2. Do you think Student A or Student B analyses the sentence most effectively? Complete the comments below.

The student who analyses the sentence most effectively is _

because _

_ _

_ _

_ _

3. Continue your chosen student answer by clearly explaining the effect of the use of language in the final sentence: 'By the time I'd got him safely tied to his stake, I was sweating.'

Selecting relevant textual detail

In order to achieve your target grade in response to Question 2, you must support your explanation of how the writer has used language with a range of relevant textual detail (i.e. quotations) and references to the text. To select and use a range of relevant textual detail, you need to:

- choose the shortest and best quotation that supports the *point* you are making

- weave short quotations, as *evidence*, into your own sentences explaining the writer's methods

- pick out particular words to *explain* in even more detail.

In your answer to Question 2, make sure that the points you make *explain* the effects created by the language choices the writer has made. Avoid making general comments that could apply to any text and focus on linking your explanation to the specific evidence you have chosen.

Look at how the following student has done this, using Point, Evidence, Explain.

Point: The writer builds up adjectives in this extract.

Evidence: For example, 'small' and 'cold' to describe the lake.

Explanation: The adjective 'small' is a short one-syllable word, emphasizing the small size of the narrator, as well as the lake, in the enormous landscape. The simple word 'cold' reminds the reader of the harshness of the Arctic environment.

Activity 4

Look at the range of quotations the student has selected in the answer on page 21. They have started to explain the effects created by these language choices.

1. Complete the annotations on separate paper to explain what effects are created by the specific examples of language chosen.

2. Circle three more relevant quotations. Write a brief annotation for each of these on separate paper, explaining how they contribute to the overall effect the writer is trying to create.

The landscape and elements are described as if they are alive. This suggests …

The use of the verb 'stumbling' emphasizes the steepness of the land and the effort the narrator has to make to climb it.

As I climbed higher, the going got tougher. I found myself stumbling over naked scree and brittle black lichen. The wind was sharp, and I was soon chilled. Clouds obscured the icecap, but I felt its freezing breath. When I took off my hat, my skull began to ache within seconds.

Behind the hiss of the wind and the chatter of the stream, the land lay silent. I passed the skeleton of a reindeer. I came to a standing stone by a small, cold lake. I stopped. I was aware of the noises around me – the wind, the water, my panting breath – but somehow they only deepened the stillness. I felt it as a physical presence. Immense. Overwhelming. I realised that this place is, and will always be, no-man's-land.

These short sentences suggest …

The writer uses language of power. The words 'immense' and 'overwhelming' suggest …

'Sharp', 'freezing' and 'chilled' suggest a harsh setting that is uncomfortable for the narrator.

The phrase 'no-man's land' suggests this is no place for people. It makes the reader think there is danger for the man.

Activity 5

1. Now look at the following extract from the student's answer to Question 2 looked at on page 18.

> **2** How does the writer use language to describe the narrator's life in the Arctic?

Annotate the response by placing a number where you find evidence of the following key features of a Grade 5 response.

1. Chooses the shortest and best quotation to support the point made.

2. Integrates short quotations into their own sentences explaining the writer's methods.

3. Picks out particular words to explain in even more detail.

2. Now write your own paragraph explaining the effects created by the quotations you circled in Activity 4.

Student A

The writer describes the narrator's life as difficult and dangerous. His body is described as 'chilled' and as soon as he takes his hat off his skull 'begins to ache'. The phrase 'within seconds' shows how quickly this happens and the word 'skull' makes the reader think of people dying in this place. The writer describes the icecap having 'freezing breath'. The personification suggests that the icecap is alive and a force against the man.

Using subject terminology accurately

In order to achieve your target grade in response to Question 2, you must use subject terminology clearly and accurately. This means that as well as identifying language features and explaining the effects these create, you should use the correct subject terminology to name them.

Activity 6

1. Look at the examples of key terms below and link them to their correct definitions. An example has been done for you.

Terms	Definitions
Simile	A literary device where strongly stressed consonants create a hissing sound
Metaphor	Repetition of initial consonants for a specific effect
Symbolism	Where an object is used to represent an abstract idea
Imagery	A word that identifies actions, thoughts, feelings or the state of being
Sibilance	Representing an idea in human form or presenting a thing as having human characteristics
Alliteration	Words that are used to modify verbs, adjectives or whole sentences
Simple sentence	A sentence which has a main clause (which could stand alone as a simple sentence) and a dependent clause (which could not stand alone as a sentence on its own)
Complex sentence	Where one thing is compared to another thing, using a connective word such as 'like' or 'as'
Personification	A word that describes a noun
Verb	A sentence made up of a single clause; it has a subject and one main verb
Adjective	A comparison showing the similarity between two quite different things where one is described as the other
Adverb	The use of figurative or other special language to convey an idea to readers

2. Look back at the annotations you completed in Activity 4 on pages 20–21. Identify any of the annotations where you could add relevant subject terminology to improve the explanations.

3. Now look back at the paragraph you wrote in Activity 5 on page 21. Did you use subject terminology correctly here? If not, redraft the paragraph on separate paper to include this.

Exam tip

Remember to avoid feature spotting in your answer. There is no value in using a key term unless you explain *how* the author is using the technique to achieve a *specific effect*.

Look again at the following source text from *Dark Matter* by Michelle Paver.

> As I climbed higher, the going got tougher. I found myself stumbling over naked scree and brittle black lichen. The wind was sharp, and I was soon chilled. Clouds obscured the icecap, but I felt its freezing breath. When I took off my hat, my skull began to ache within seconds.
>
> Behind the hiss of the wind and the chatter of the stream, the land lay silent. I passed the skeleton of a reindeer. I came to a standing stone by a small, cold lake. I stopped. I was aware of the noises around me – the wind, the water, my panting breath – but somehow they only deepened the stillness. I felt it as a physical presence. Immense. Overwhelming. I realised that this place is, and will always be, no-man's-land.

Activity 7

1. Pick two key terms from the list on page 22, which you can find in *Dark Matter*, the text above. Find an example for each of these. Explain why you think Paver, the author, has included them.

   [Point] Paver uses _____

   [Evidence] For example, _____

   _____

   [Explain] This develops a sense of _____

   _____

   [Point] The writer also uses _____

   [Evidence] For example, _____

   _____

   [Explain] This develops a sense of _____

   _____

2. Now identify one final language feature and analyse the effect it creates, using 'Point, Evidence, Explanation' to write your own complete paragraph on separate paper.

Exam tip

Using the 'Point, Evidence, Explanation' model will ensure you write clear explanations with a range of relevant textual detail in the exam.

Now read the following source text and complete Activity 8 on page 25. The following extract is taken from a novel about the famous detective Sherlock Holmes, written by Anthony Horowitz and published in 2011. In this extract, the narrator, Dr Watson, describes his experience as he and Sherlock Holmes chase the criminal Harriman, who is escaping in a horse and carriage.

The House of Silk by Anthony Horowitz

This was no night for a chase. The snow was sweeping at us horizontally, punching at us in a series of continuous bursts. I could not begin to understand how Holmes could see, for every time I tried to peer into the darkness I was instantly blinded and
5 my cheeks were already numb with cold. But there was Harriman, no more than fifty yards ahead of us. I heard him cry out with vexation, heard the lash of his whip. Holmes was sitting in front of me, crouched forward, holding the reins with both hands, keeping his balance only with his feet. Every pothole threatened to throw
10 him out. The slightest curve caused us to skid madly across the icy surface of the road. I wondered if the **splinter bars** could possibly hold, and in my mind's eye I saw **imminent** catastrophe as our steed, excited by the chase, ended up dashing us to pieces. The hill was steep and it was as if we were plunging into a
15 chasm with the snow swirling all around us and the wind sucking us down.

Forty yards, thirty… somehow we were managing to close the gap between us. The hooves of the other horses were thundering down, the wheels of the **curricle** madly spinning, the entire
20 structure rattling and shaking as if it would tear itself apart at any time. Harriman was aware of us now. I saw him glance back, his white hair a mad halo around his head. He reached for something. Too late did I see what it was. There was tiny flash of red, a gunshot that was almost lost in the **cacophony** of the chase.
25 I heard the bullet strike wood. It had missed Holmes by inches and me by even less. The closer we were, the easier a target we became. And yet still we hurtled down.

Glossary

splinter bar: a crossbar in a carriage or coach that supports the springs

imminent: likely to happen at any moment

curricle: a small lightweight two-wheeled carriage

cacophony: a harsh discordant mixture of sounds

8 minutes

Activity 8

Example Exam Question

2 Look in detail at this extract from lines 7 to 21 of the source.

How does the writer use language to describe the narrator, Watson's, experience of the chase?

You could include the writer's choice of:

- words and phrases
- language features and techniques
- sentence forms.

> Holmes was sitting in front of me, crouched forward, holding the reins with both hands, keeping his balance only with his feet. Every pothole threatened to throw him out. The slightest curve caused us to skid madly across the icy surface of the road. I wondered if the splinter bars could possibly hold, and in my mind's eye I saw imminent catastrophe as our steed, excited by the chase, ended up dashing us to pieces. The hill was steep and it was as if we were plunging into a chasm with the snow swirling all around us and the wind sucking us down.
>
> Forty yards, thirty…somehow we were managing to close the gap between us. The hooves of the other horses were thundering down, the wheels of the curricle madly spinning, the entire structure rattling and shaking as if it would tear itself apart at any time.

Write your answer to the question in the space below and continue on blank paper. In the exam you will be given at least a page and a half to write your response, but you don't have to use all the space.

Remember that for a Grade 5 response you must:

- show *clear* understanding when you *explain* the effects of the writer's choices of language

- use subject terminology *accurately* when writing about language

- select and use a *range* of *relevant* quotations and examples.

Progress check

Look back at your answer to Activity 8. You could annotate your answer to pick out the evidence that shows any of the following skills:

- shows *clear* understanding when explaining the effects of the writer's choices of language

- selects and uses a *range* of *relevant* textual detail i.e. quotations and examples

- uses subject terminology *clearly* and *accurately* when writing about language.

		Check ✔
Analysing how writers use language to achieve effects and influence readers	I can make simple comments on the effect of language.	
	I can *explain clearly* the effects of the writer's choices of language.	
Supporting your ideas with appropriate textual references	I can select simple references or textual details.	
	I can select and use a *range* of *relevant* textual details.	
Using relevant subject terminology to support your views	I mention simple subject terminology when writing about language.	
	I make *clear* and *accurate* use of subject terminology when writing about language.	

Question 3

Using structure to achieve effects and influence readers

This question assesses your ability to analyse the effects of a writer's use of structure. To produce a Grade 5 response you will need to:

- show *clear* understanding when you *explain* the effects of a writer's choice of structural features

- select and use a *range* of *relevant* examples

- make *clear* and *accurate* use of subject terminology when writing about structure.

Look back at the qualities of a Grade 5 response to Question 3 listed above. Notice the words in italics which indicate what distinguishes a good response from a weaker answer.

You will now explore each of these key skills to help you write the best possible answer to Question 3. These are the same skills you used for Question 2, but you are now applying these to the analysis of *structure* rather than language.

What is structure?

The key to success in this question is to be clear what is meant by **structure**. What should you identify in any unseen extract?

The structure of a text means 'how it has been built'.

	With a house, this might mean the following:	With a text, this might mean the following:
What does it look like overall?	• standing back and considering the shape of the whole building	• standing back and considering the development and mood of the whole text and its effect on the reader
How is it built? What are its layers?	• looking closer to notice the different levels, for example, foundations, floor 1, floor 2, attic, the roof	• looking closer to notice paragraphs, their focus and how they are organized
What is it made of? What are the 'ingredients'?	• moving closer to look at the bricks and mortar	• moving in to look at sentences and their structure

Key skills you must demonstrate when answering Question 3 are:

- *selecting* relevant examples of structural features throughout the passage

- *commenting* on them and *analysing* them.

Establishing clear understanding

Before you explore the structure of a text you must ensure you understand:

- the events in the text – what is it about?

- words in the text – is there any unfamiliar vocabulary? Is it explained in the glossary?

If you launch into your answer without establishing these basics, it's easy to lose focus on the text and question.

The following extract is an early passage from the novella 'The Birds' by Daphne du Maurier in which a community is attacked by birds who go on to attack the whole country. The story inspired the later horror film by Alfred Hitchcock.

'The Birds' by Daphne du Maurier

Even the air in the small bedroom had turned chill: a draft came under the skirting of the door, blowing upon the bed. Nat drew the blanket round him, leaned closer to the back of his sleeping wife, and stayed wakeful, watchful, aware of **misgiving** without cause.

5   Then he heard the tapping on the window. There was no creeper on the cottage walls to break loose and scratch upon the pane. He listened, and the tapping continued until, irritated by the sound, Nat got out of bed and went to the window. He opened it, and as he did so something brushed his hand, jabbing at his knuckles, grazing the skin. Then he saw the flutter of
10   the wings and it was gone, over the roof, behind the cottage.

It was a bird; what kind of bird he could not tell. The wind must have driven it to shelter on the sill.

He shut the window and went back to bed but, feeling his knuckles wet, put his mouth to the scratch. The bird had drawn blood. Frightened, he
15   supposed, and bewildered, the bird, seeking shelter, had stabbed at him in the darkness. Once more he settled himself to sleep.

Presently the tapping came again, this time more forceful, more insistent, and now his wife woke at the sound and, turning in the bed, said to him, "See to the window, Nat, it's rattling."

20   "I've already seen to it," he told her; "there's some bird there trying to get in. Can't you hear the wind? It's blowing from the east, driving the birds to shelter."

"Send them away," she said, "I can't sleep with that noise."

He went to the window for the second time, and now when he opened it,
25   there was not one bird upon the sill but half a dozen; they flew straight into his face, attacking him.

He shouted, striking out at them with his arms, scattering them; like the first one, they flew over the roof and disappeared. Quickly he let the window fall and latched it.

30   "Did you hear that?" he said. "They went for me. Tried to peck my eyes."

He stood by the window, peering into the darkness, and could see nothing. His wife, heavy with sleep, murmured from the bed.

"I'm not making it up," he said, angry at her suggestion. "I tell you the birds were on the sill, trying to get into the room."

35 Suddenly a frightened cry came from the room across the passage where the children slept.

"It's Jill," said his wife, roused at the sound, sitting up in bed. "Go to her, see what's the matter."

Nat lit the candle, but when he opened the bedroom door to cross the
40 passage the draft blew out the flame.

There came a second cry of terror, this time from both children, and stumbling into their room, he felt the beating of wings about him in the darkness. The window was wide open. Through it came the birds, hitting first the ceiling and the walls, then swerving in midflight, turning to the
45 children in their beds.

"It's all right, I'm here," shouted Nat, and the children flung themselves, screaming, upon him, while in the darkness the birds rose and dived and came for him again.

"What is it, Nat, what's happened?" his wife called from the further
50 bedroom, and swiftly he pushed the children through the door to the passage and shut it upon them, so that he was alone now in their bedroom with the birds.

Glossary

misgiving: feeling uncomfortable or uneasy for no particular reason

Activity 1

Write two sentences to summarize the events described in the passage.

Writing about structure

When answering Question 3 in the exam, you should consider these three key aspects of structure:

- **the sequence through a passage:** (introduction, development, summary, conclusion), repetition, threads, patterns, motifs

- **shifts in ideas and perspectives:** (for example, movement from big to small, place to place, outside to inside), narrative perspectives, one point in time to another

- **coherence and cohesion:** the way a piece of writing links together in terms of vocabulary, sentences and paragraphs, for example, connections and links across paragraphs, links within paragraphs, topic sentences.

Look at the following example Question 3 about the source text you have read on pages 28–29, 'The Birds'.

Notice the key words that have been circled by a student. Notice how you are being asked to consider *what the writer is doing* and *how the passage is built* from its opening through to its end.

> **Exam tip**
>
> When answering Question 3 in the exam you need to use subject terminology clearly and accurately. Think about how you can use these terms when explaining the effects of these different structural features.

Example Exam Question

3 You now need to think about the whole of the source.

This text is from the early section of a novel.

How has the writer used structure to create an atmosphere of suspense?

You could write about:

- what the writer focuses your attention on at the beginning

- how and why the writer changes this focus as the extract develops

- any other structural features that interest you.

The overall effect

Question 3 asks you to think about the whole of the source text. Consider:

- how the text has been structured to make an impact on the reader.

- how the question states the type of mood or atmosphere created in the source text. Be aware that this could change as the text develops.

In the example Question 3 above, you have been asked to explore how the writer has used structure to create an atmosphere of suspense.

Activity 2

If the question states the mood or atmosphere created in the text, it can be helpful to think of synonyms for this that you could use in your answer.

1. Re-read the source text extract on pages 28–29 and for each paragraph choose one of the words below to describe the mood of that paragraph. For some paragraphs you might want to choose more than one word.

> Tension   Uncertainty   Anticipation
>
> Terror
>
> Excitement   Confusion   Fear

Paragraph 1: _____

Paragraph 2: _____

Paragraph 3: _____

Paragraph 4: _____

Paragraph 5: _____

Paragraph 6: _____

Paragraph 7: _____

Paragraph 8: _____

Paragraph 9: _____

Paragraph 10: _____

Paragraph 11: _____

Paragraph 12: _____

Paragraph 13: _____

Paragraph 14: _____

Paragraph 15: _____

Paragraph 16: _____

Paragraph 17: _____

2. Look at the words you have chosen and consider how the mood changes in the text extract. Using the following symbols, mark on the extract the paragraphs that:

↑ gradually build up suspense   ↓ gradually decrease suspense

∿ alternate between one mood and another.

Understanding the sequence of a text

Once you have a clear overview of the overall effect of the text, you should look carefully at the sections of the text and how it is organized.

Activity 3

Look back at the source text on pages 28–29 and fill in the boxes below.
Do you think it fits best into four or five sections? Give each section a title and brief explanation. The first two have been done for you.

Section 1

Title: _Setting the scene_ Explanation: _The bedroom seems quiet but uneasy._

Section 2

Title: _The first tap at the window_ Explanation: _Nat sees the bird, opens the window and is injured. His sleepy wife isn't concerned._

Section 3

Title: _____ Explanation: _____

Section 4

Title: _____ Explanation: _____

Section 5

Title: _____ Explanation: _____

Other people in your class may have divided the text into a different number of sections. What matters is that you can identify logical sections and consider how the writer guides the reader's response – there is not one right answer.

Activity 4

1. The sound of a cry is another detail that the writer repeats in the source text. Pick out the two quotations where this is mentioned:

    Quotation 1: _____

    Quotation 2: _____

2. On blank paper, write a brief paragraph explaining how the repetition of this detail helps to create an atmosphere of suspense.

Identifying shifts in ideas and perspectives

When you explore the structure of a text you need to consider:

- what the writer focuses your attention on

- how and why this focus changes as the text develops.

The narrative pace of the section, that is, how quickly or slowly the writer takes the reader through the action, can also be affected by these shifts in focus.

Activity 5

Note down in each box below what the writer focuses your attention on as the story develops. Notice the movement between different settings. You might want to consider the following settings:

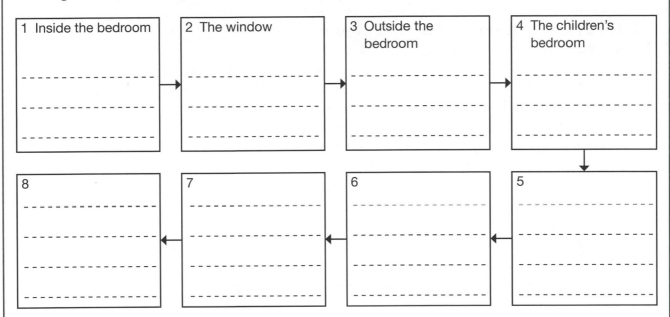

1. In each box, write a sentence commenting on the narrative pace of that section of the text.

2. When in the story do you realize that children have let the birds in?

3. Can you identify the early clue given in the first paragraph that hints at this? Write it below.

Identifying connections and links

When answering Question 3 in the exam you need to:

- identify how different parts of the text are linked

- explain the effects created by these connections

- look for links between paragraphs, for example, the use of topic sentences or dialogue links.

Activity 6

1. Re-read the final section of the source text, 'The Birds' extract. Annotate this to identify:

   - use of time connectives to link past and previous actions

   - dialogue

   - contrasts, for example, inside/outside, people/birds, together/alone.

   > There came a second cry of terror, this time from both children, and stumbling into their room, he felt the beating of wings about him in the darkness. The window was wide open. Through it came the birds, hitting first the ceiling and the walls, then swerving in midflight, turning to the children in their beds.
   >
   > "It's all right, I'm here," shouted Nat, and the children flung themselves, screaming, upon him, while in the darkness the birds rose and dived and came for him again.
   >
   > "What is it, Nat, what's happened?" his wife called from the further bedroom, and swiftly he pushed the children through the door to the passage and shut it upon them, so that he was alone now in their bedroom with the birds.

2. Write a paragraph explaining how the structural features of this text contribute to the atmosphere of suspense.

Using subject terminology accurately

When we explore language features in a text (the other part of this Assessment Objective, assessed in Question 2), we have a number of terms that we can use to describe them (see page 22).

When we write about structure, however, we need to use completely different language. Because structure is about changes from one feature to another, we are likely to use verbs much more often. So we might write:

At this point the focus *shifts*...

Or

The writer *speeds up* the action here in order to...

This is because the writer uses structural features to guide us through the text so we must describe them as actions.

Activity 7

Look back at your answers to Activity 5 on page 33. Using these notes, write two paragraphs explaining how the writer has used structure to create an atmosphere of suspense.

Remember to use relevant terminology and examples from the text.

Exam tip

The following phrases can be used to comment on structure in the exam. Think about how the verbs shown in italics help you to identify how the writer is guiding the reader through the text.

- The writer *develops/builds*...
- The focus *shifts*...
- The action *moves*...
- The scene *switches*...
- The focus *narrows down*...
- The focus *widens*...
- The writer *returns to*...
- The pace *increases/slows*...
- The writer *contrasts*...

Writing your answer

Now read Student A's response to the example Question 3 on page 30.

Student A

The extract describes the build-up to a bird attack and the writer has structured it so that the focus shifts backwards and forwards between the risk of the bird outside and the relative safety of the house. The atmosphere of suspense is gradually built up by the man at first feeling uneasy, his opening and shutting of the window on hearing the bird and gaining an injury and finally hearing his children scream and realizing that the birds have been let in. This event was foreshadowed earlier in the passage by the man feeling a breeze through his door. By the end the reader realizes that our uneasiness at the beginning was correct and that the birds had been able to get in to the house near the children. The birds outside are now inside and humans and birds are no longer separate there which leads to a terrifying attack.

Activity 8

1. Annotate Student A's answer, using three different colours, to identify where the student has:

   - clearly explained how the writer's choice of structural features create an atmosphere of suspense

   - selected relevant examples from the text

   - accurately used subject terminology related to the structure and atmosphere of the writing.

2. Now identify at least two further points to add to Student A's response. Continue their answer in the space below. You do not need to use quotations.

Activity 9

Now read the next section of 'The Birds'. Annotate the source text below to explore how the writer has structured the text to interest you as a reader.

This section of the text starts at the high point of the tension and then gradually becomes calmer. Remember to look for the structural features that the writer uses to lessen the tension. Think about:

- the narrative pace and how this changes

- the way the writer creates pace

- echoes and references to the earlier period of suspense before the birds arrived

- the climax of the passage

- any other structural features you can identify, such as changes in setting or focus.

He seized a blanket from the nearest bed and, using it as a weapon, flung it to right and left about him in the air. He felt the thud of bodies, heard the fluttering of wings, but they were not yet defeated, for again and again they returned to the assault, jabbing his hands, his head, the little stabbing beaks sharp as pointed forks. The blanket became a weapon of defence; he wound it about his head, and then in greater darkness beat at the birds with his bare hands. He dared not stumble to the door and open it, lest in doing so the birds should follow him.

How long he fought with them in the darkness he could not tell, but at last the beating of the wings about him lessened and then withdrew, and through the density of the blanket he was aware of light. He waited, listened; there was no sound except the fretful crying of one of the children from the bedroom beyond. The fluttering, the whirring of the wings had ceased.

He took the blanket from his head and stared about him. The cold gray morning light exposed the room. Dawn and the open window had called the living birds; the dead lay on the floor. Nat gazed at the little corpses, shocked and horrified. They were all small birds, none of any size; there must have been fifty of them lying there upon the floor.

15 minutes

Activity 10

Look back at the annotations you made in Activity 9 on the previous page. Refer to the text on page 37 and these annotations as you write your answer to the following example Question 3.

Example Exam Question

3 This text follows on from the opening of 'The Birds'.

How has the writer structured the text to interest you as a reader?

You could write about:

- what the writer focuses your attention on at the beginning
- how and why the writer changes this focus as the extract develops
- any other structural features that interest you.

Exam tip

Think about how you use your time when answering Question 3 in the exam. You should make sure that you cover each of the question's bullet points in your answer. Try to make at least one point about:

- how the text begins
- the sequence through the text
- shifts in focus
- structural features used to create links
- how the text ends.

This passage is from the opening of the novel *The Midwich Cuckoos* by
John Wyndham. Here, we are introduced by the narrator, Richard, to
events that have happened in a village. The whole village has become
unconscious after a large silver object has landed there. When they wake a
day later everyone is unharmed – except that all the women in the village
are pregnant.

The Midwich Cuckoos by John Wyndham

No other evidence has been produced to suggest that on that
Monday, until late in the evening, Midwich was anything but normal.
Just, in fact, as it had appeared to be when Janet and I set off for
London. And yet, on Tuesday the 27th…

5 We locked the car, climbed the gate, and started over the field of
stubble keeping well into the hedge. At the end of that we came to
another field of stubble and bore leftwards across it, slightly uphill. It
was a big field with a good hedge on the far side, and we had to go
further left to find a gate we could climb. Half-way across the pasture
10 beyond brought us to the top of the rise, and we were able to look
out across Midwich – not that much of it was visible for trees, but we
could see a couple of wisps of greyish smoke lazily rising, and the
church spire sticking up by the elms. Also, in the middle of the next
field I could see four or five cows lying down, apparently asleep.

15 I am not a countryman, I only live there, but I remember thinking
rather far back in my mind that there was something not quite right
about that. Cows folded up, chewing cud, yes, commonly enough
but cows lying down fast asleep, well, no. But it did not do more at
the time than give me a vague feeling of something out of true. We
20 went on.

We climbed the fence of the field where the cows were and started
across that, too.

A voice hallooed at us, away on the left. I looked round and made
out a khaki-clad figure in the middle of the next field. He was calling
25 something intelligible, but the way he was waving his stick was
without doubt a sign for us to go back. I stopped.

'Oh, come on, Richard. He's miles away,' said Janet impatiently, and
began to run on ahead.

I still hesitated, looking at the figure who was now waving his stick
30 more energetically than ever, and shouting more loudly, though
no more intelligibly. I decided to follow Janet. She had perhaps
twenty yards start of me by now, and then, just as I started off, she
staggered, collapsed without a sound, and lay quite still…

I stopped dead. That was involuntary. If she had gone down with a
35 twisted ankle, or had simply tripped I should have run on, to her. But
this was so sudden and so complete that for a moment I thought,
idiotically, that she had been shot.

The stop was only momentary. Then I went on again.

Dimly I was aware of the man away on the left still shouting, but I did
40 not bother about him. I hurried towards her…

But I did not reach her.

I went out so completely that I never even saw the ground come up to hit me.

Chapter 2

45 As I said, all was normal in Midwich on the 26th. I have looked into the matter extensively, and can tell you where practically everyone was, and what they were doing that evening.

Activity 11

1. Take five minutes to read and annotate the source text *The Midwich Cuckoos* on pages 39–40.

2. Now spend 10 minutes writing your answer to the question below, using the writing space provided and continuing on blank paper. Remember, in the exam you will be given at least a page and a half to write your response, but you don't have to use all this space.

Example Exam Question

3 You now need to think about the whole of the source.

This text is from the opening of a novel.

How has the writer structured the text to effectively interest the reader in the strange events at Midwich?

You could write about:

- the characters' journey

- how the writer introduces information about characters, time and place

- any other structural features that interest you.

Activity 11 *continued*

Progress check

Now that you have practised the skills needed for a Grade 5 response to Question 3, carry out the progress check below. Use three highlighter pens of different colours to highlight sections of your answer to Activity 11 to show where you have satisfied each of the criteria for Grade 5.

		Check ✔
Explaining how writers use structure to achieve effects and influence readers	I can clearly identify relevant structural features.	
	I can explain clearly the effects of the writer's choice of structural features.	
Using relevant subject terminology to support your views	I can make clear and accurate use of subject terminology relating to structural features.	
Supporting your ideas with appropriate textual references	I can support my ideas with a range of relevant examples.	

Question 4

Evaluate texts critically

Question 4 assesses your ability to **evaluate** the effectiveness of a text. This means you must come to an informed personal judgement about a text and the choices made by the writer.

To produce a Grade 5 response you must consistently show that you can:

- evaluate *clearly* the effect on the reader
- show *clear* understanding of the writer's methods
- select a range of *relevant* textual references
- make a *clear* and *relevant* response to the focus of the statement.

Notice the words in italics which indicate the skills that distinguish a Grade 5 response to Question 4 from a weaker answer.

The following question is an example of Question 4 in the exam:

Example Exam Question

> **4** Focus this part of your answer on the second half of the source, from line 23 to the end.
>
> On reading this section of the text, a student said, 'The writer makes you understand André's fascination with the powerline and the exciting life it represents to him. It is as though you can see through the eyes of this child.'
>
> To what extent do you agree?
>
> In your response, you could:
>
> - write about your own impressions of André
> - evaluate how the writer has conveyed his fascination with the powerline
> - support your opinions with quotations from the text.

In your answer to this question, you must show that you:

- understand and evaluate the effects of a text on the reader
- can identify and explain the tools used to do this – the writer's methods
- can make a clear and relevant response to the focus of the statement.

Evaluating the effect on the reader

Writers of fiction know the ideas they want to convey about the characters, setting and situations they create. This is called the writer's intention. Their skill lies in how language or structural features, are used to create these effects on the reader.

In Question 4 you will be presented with a quotation from a student. This will relate to a specified section of the source text and give the student's judgement about the author's intentions or the effect on the reader. You will need to consider how far you agree with the student's judgement.

Activity 1

1. Remind yourself of the student's quotation presented in the example Question 4 on page 43 and describe what the writer is conveying. Here is the quotation again:

> 'The writer makes you understand André's fascination with the powerline and the exciting life it represents to him. It is as though you can see through the eyes of this child.'

2. Focusing on the second half of the source, from line 22 to the end, highlight quotations that:

   - convey André's fascination with the powerline and what is represents

   - convey a child's viewpoint.

This extract is taken from a short story about a South African boy living in an isolated area, who can see a large electricity pylon and powerline from his house.

'Power' by Jack Cope

André was ten and he knew volts were electricity and the line took power by a short cut far across country. It worked gold mines, it lit towns, and hauled trains and drove machinery somewhere out beyond. The power station was in the town ten
5 miles on the other side of his father's place and the great line simply jumped right over them without stopping.

André filled the empty spaces in his life by imagining things. Often he was a jet plane and roared around the house and along the paths with his arms outspread. He saw an Everest
10 film once and for a long time he was **Hillary** or **Tensing**, or both, conquering a mountain. There were no mountains so he conquered the roof of the house which wasn't very high and was made of red-painted tin. But he reached the summit and planted a flag on the lightning conductor. When he got

15   down his mother hit his legs with a **quince switch** for being naughty.

Another time he conquered the **koppie**. It took him the whole afternoon to get there and back and it was not as exciting as he expected, being less steep than it looked from a distance,
20   so he did not need his rope and pick. Also, he found a cow had beaten him to the summit.

He thought of conquering one of the powerline towers. It had everything, the danger especially, and studying it from all sides he guessed he could make the summit without touching a live
25   wire. But he was not as disobedient as all that, and he knew if he so much as went inside the barbed-wire fence his mother would skin him with the quince, not to mention his father. There were peaks which had to remain unconquered.

He used to lie and listen to the marvellous hum of the
30   powerline, the millions of volts flowing invisible and beyond all one's ideas along the copper wires that hung so smooth and light from ties of crinkled white china looking like Chinese lanterns up against the sky. Faint cracklings and murmurs and rushes of sound would sometimes come from the powerline,
35   and at night he was sure he saw soft blue flames lapping and trembling on the wires as if they were only half peeping out of that fierce river of volts. The flames danced and their voices chattered to him of a mystery.

In the early morning when the mist was rising and the first
40   sun's rays were shooting underneath it, the powerline sparkled like a tremendous spiderweb. It took his thoughts away into a magical distance, far – far off among gigantic machines and busy factories. That was where the world opened up. So he loved the powerline dearly. It made a door through the
45   distance for his thoughts. It was like him except that it never slept, and while he was dreaming it went on without stopping, crackling faintly and murmuring. Its electricity hauled up the mine skips from the heart of the earth, hurtled huge green rail units along their shining lines, and thundered day and night in
50   the factories.

Glossary

Hillary: Edmund Hillary, one of the first men to reach the summit of Mount Everest

Tensing: Tensing Norgay, one of the first men to reach the summit of Everest

quince switch: a flexible cane cut from a quince tree

koppie: a small hill on South African grazing land

Understanding the writer's methods

When answering Question 4, you need to:

- identify the writer's intentions
- consider the student statement
- consider how far you agree.

This means exploring how the writer's choices contribute to the authorial intention that the student statement has identified and evaluating their effectiveness.

Remind yourself of the example Question 4.

Example Exam Question

> **4** Focus this part of your answer on the second half of the source, from line 23 to the end.
>
> On reading this section of the text, a student said, 'The writer makes you understand André's fascination with the powerline and the exciting life it represents to him. It is as though you can see through the eyes of this child.'
>
> To what extent do you agree?
>
> In your response, you could:
>
> - write about your own impressions of André
>
> - evaluate how the writer has conveyed his fascination with the powerline
>
> - support your opinions with quotations from the text.

Look at the annotations that Student A has made on the opening paragraph of the specified section of the source text. These focus on Student A's own impression of André and how this is created.

The word 'conquering' suggests André's child-like view of imagining he is an explorer like Hilary.

This line shows André's childish excitement about danger.

The child is more worried about what his mother will do than the real danger of the tower.

He thought of conquering one of the powerline towers. It had everything, the danger especially, and studying it from all sides he guessed he could make the summit without touching a live wire. But he was not as disobedient as all that, and he knew if he so much as went inside the barbed-wire fence his mother would skin him with the quince, not to mention his father. There were peaks which had to remain unconquered.

The word 'disobedient' is one linked to children not doing what they are told rather than adults.

In the exam, the student statement presented in Question 4 could focus on different aspects of the source text, for example, the writer's creation of: character   setting   mood   atmosphere

The question asks you to what extent you agree with the student statement. Use the question to explain why you agree, and disagree with evidence from the text. Look at both language features and structural features.

Here, the focus of your answer is on the writer's characterization of André. Remind yourself of the different techniques writers can use to create a sense of character:

voice   dialogue   vocabulary   imagery

language features   structural features, for example, contrasts, repetition

Exam tip

When answering Question 4, do not comment on what is *not* in the text. You are analysing the tools used by the writer, rather than commenting on what is *not* there. For example, in the defined extract, there is no dialogue so this does not need to be mentioned.

Activity 2

Look back at the quotations you identified in Activity 1. For each row of the table below, complete the unfinished point and then add your own evaluative statements, drawing on the examples you have identified.

Techniques	How it supports the student's statement: 'The writer makes you understand André's fascination with the powerline and the exciting life it represents to him. It is as though you can see through the eyes of this child.'
Language features: vocabulary, imagery, dialogue. *Identify phrases that describe the look of the lines, their energy and what they represent. Notice words that convey them as alive.*	The vocabulary used to describe why André doesn't climb the powerline shows his child's perspective. It contrasts the appeal of the 'danger' to his confidence, for example: 'he could make the summit without touching a live wire', with his fear of being skinned 'with the quince switch' if he is caught. Similes used to describe the powerline are 'looking like Chinese lanterns' and 'like a tremendous spiderweb'. These images create a sense of... ------------------------------ ------------------------------
Structural features: contrasts, repetition, time connectives. *Think carefully about André's home and how the pylon links to the wider world.*	The penultimate paragraph describes André in bed listening to the 'marvellous hum' of the powerline. However, it then says he sees 'blue flames lapping and trembling on the wires' at night. The final paragraph begins with a time connective, 'In the early morning', to describe the powerline at dawn, emphasizing André's fascination with the powerline both in the morning and at night. The writer contrasts the isolation of André's home with... ------------------------------ ------------------------------

Responding to the focus of the statement

In the exam, stick to the suggested timings rather than amount of space given. For Question 4, you will have 20 minutes. Follow this plan:

write a brief introduction: make a summative statement presenting your personal judgement about how far you agree with the student's statement

evaluate the techniques the writer uses to achieve their intention or create specific effects as described in the student's statement. Aim to make two points about the language features used and two points about the structural features

summarize your evaluation of the writer's success in achieving the stated aim.

Read the source text on page 50 and look at the example Question 4 below.

Example Exam Question

4 On reading this section of the text, a student said, 'The writer conveys the setting and events as extraordinary and shocking.'

To what extent do you agree?

In your response, you could:

- write about your own impressions of the setting
- evaluate how the writer has conveyed the extraordinary and shocking nature of the events described
- support your opinions with quotations from the text.

Activity 3

1. Read the opening section of answers by Student A and Student B to this question. Using different colours, highlight:

   • clear points that give the student's personal judgement in relation to the statement given in the question

   • references to details from the text to support the student's personal judgement.

Student A

In the short, one-sentence paragraph that opens the extract the writer describes a normal everyday scene, stating the time of day and the season and describing the everyday event of a red London bus 'crossing Waterloo bridge'. However, the strange and magical events the writer then goes on to describe transform this into an extraordinary setting.

Student B

The author makes the reader believe that everything is normal at the beginning of this passage because there is a normal scene of children on a school bus in a city. However, things become stranger and stranger as the mood changes from a feeling of normality to make the setting seem more shocking later, when the river runs backwards and strange people are riding on it. There are many events and descriptions in this scene that are out of the ordinary such as Cleopatra's needle glowing red and chariots riding down the Thames.

2. Which student's response do you think is better? Give reasons for your choice.

This extract is from the opening of the novel *Tanglewreck* by Jeanette Winterson. It is set in modern-day London.

Tanglewreck by Jeanette Winterson

At six forty-five one summer morning, a red London bus was crossing Waterloo Bridge.

A group of school children, sitting at the back, were copying each other's homework and fighting, when one of them looked out of
5 the window, across the river, to **Cleopatra's Needle**, and saw something very strange.

The boy elbowed his friend. The dark finger of ancient Egypt was pointing towards the sky as it always did, but today the tip of the **obelisk** was glowing bright red, as it had when it was new and
10 painted and glorious, four thousand years ago, in the Temple of the Sun.

'Look,' said the boy, 'look!'

Riding the river as though it were a road was a **phalanx** of chariots and horsemen.

15 The white horses were pulled up on their haunches; the nodding ostrich plumes on their head-collars rose and fell; the fan bearers came forward, the troops stood at ease, and above the kneeling priests was the **Pharoah** himself, inspecting his new monument from a burnished car.

20 Other people turned to stare at the **mirage**, and the bus driver slowed down, though he did not quite stop; he seemed to be hovering over Time.

In the slowed-down silence no one spoke and nothing moved – except for the river, which to all observation was running
25 backwards.

Then, from downstream, there was a sudden terrible crack, like the sky breaking. A cone of wind hit the bus, knocking it sideways over the bridge and shattering glass across the seats where the children were sitting.

30 The bus should have crashed down into the river, but instead the wind whirled through the punched-in windows and lifted the bus high above the bridge and out towards the obelisk.

A great wave of water swelled up against the stone piers of the bridge, battering the concrete underside with such force that part
35 of the supporting wall was torn away.

As the tidal wave slammed back down on to the water, the river resumed its normal flow. At the same second the bus spun crazily into the line of chariots. On impact, bus, chariots and horsemen vanished, leaving nothing behind but traces of red-gold sun on the
40 surface of the water.

Big Ben struck seven.

Glossary

Cleopatra's Needle: the Ancient Egyptian pillar in Westminster, London

obelisk: a tapering stone pillar

phalanx: a group of people or things of a similar type forming a compact body

Pharoah: an Ancient Egyptian king

mirage: bent light rays that produce an illusion of an image

Activity 4

1. a Re-read the source text on page 50 and underline quotations that suggest an ordinary setting and everyday events.

  b In a different colour, underline quotations that agree with the student statement: 'The writer conveys the setting and events as extraordinary and shocking.'

2. Decide to what extent you agree that the writer conveys the setting and events as extraordinary and shocking. Mark your personal judgement on the scale below.

Agree a little   Strongly agree

3. a Identify examples of language and structural features used by the writer to convey the setting and events in the text. You should highlight these in the source text on page 50.

  b Choose the most effective examples of language features and structural features and add these to the table below.

Techniques	How techniques support or conflict with the student's statement: 'The writer conveys the setting and events as extraordinary and shocking.'
Language features: vocabulary, imagery, dialogue	
Structural features: contrasts, repetition, time connectives	

Exam tip

References to evidence from the text should support your critical evaluation of how the writer has achieved the effects stated in the question. In your answer to Question 4, you could use some of the following phrases to help you to evaluate the text.

'The writer makes...'

'This makes the reader...'

'We are shocked by...'

'As we read this part, we feel...'

'The impact of this is...'

Activity 5

Write your answer to the example Question 4, about *Tanglewreck*, below.

Example Exam Question

4 On reading this section of the text, a student said, 'The writer conveys the setting and events as extraordinary and shocking.'

To what extent do you agree?

In your response, you could:

- write about your own impressions of the setting

- evaluate how the writer has conveyed the extraordinary and shocking nature of the events described

- support your opinions with quotations from the text.

In your answer, remember to:

- start with a statement about how far you agree with the student's statement

- evaluate the techniques the writer uses to achieve their intention as described in the student's statement:

  – make two points about the different language features used

  – make two points about the different structural features

- write a brief conclusion – summarize your evaluation of how the writer conveys ideas.

Write your answer to the question in the space provided and continue on blank paper. In the exam you will be given up to four pages to write your response.

20 minutes

Activity 6

Read the source text on pages 54–55 and answer the example Question 4 below.

Example Exam Question

4 Focus this part of your answer on the first four paragraphs of the extract, from line 1 to 37.

After reading this section of the text, a student said: 'I really like the way the writer builds up a feeling of suspense in this part of the text. It is almost like the reader is waiting for the accident to happen.'

To what extent do you agree?

In your response, you should:

- write about your own impressions of the mood created

- evaluate how the writer has built a feeling of suspense

- support your opinions with quotations from the text.

Write your answer to the question in the space provided and continue on blank paper. In the exam you will be given up to four pages to write your response.

This text is taken from the novel *Until It's Over* by Nicci French, published in 2007. In this extract Astrid, a cycle courier who works in London, is cycling home.

> ### *Until It's Over* by Nicci French
>
> I had cycled around London for week after week, month after month, and I knew that one day I would have an accident. The only question was, which kind? One of the other messengers had been heading along Regent Street at speed
> 5   when a taxi had swung out to make a U-turn without looking. Or, at least, without looking for a bike, because people don't look for bikes. Don had hit the side of the taxi full on and woken up in hospital unable to recall his own name.
>
> There's a pub, the Horse and Jockey, where a whole bunch
> 10   of us despatch riders meet up on Friday evenings and drink and gossip and share stories and laugh about tumbles. But every few months or so there'd be worse news. The most recent was about the man who was cycling down near the Elephant and Castle. He was alongside a lorry that turned left
> 15   without indicating and cut the corner. That's when the gap between the lorry and the kerb shrinks from about three feet to about three inches. All you can do is get off the road. But in that case there was an iron railing in the way. The next time I cycled past I saw that people had taped bunches of flowers
> 20   to it.
>
> When these accidents happen, sometimes it's the cyclist's fault and sometimes it isn't. I've heard stories of bus drivers deliberately ramming bikes. I've seen plenty of cyclists who think that traffic lights don't apply to them. But the person
> 25   on the bike always comes off second best. Which is why you should wear a helmet and try to stay away from lorries and always assume that the driver is a blind, stupid psychopath.
>
> Even so, I knew that one day I would have an accident. There were so many different kinds, and I thought the most likely
> 30   was the one that was hardest to avoid or plan against. So it proved. But I never thought it would take place within thirty yards of my own house. As I turned into Maitland Road, I was about to swing my leg over the cross-bar. I was forty-five seconds from a hot shower and in my mind I was already off
> 35   the bike and indoors, after six hours in the saddle, when a car door opened into the road in front of me, like the wing of a metal bird, and I hit it.
>
> There was no time for me to respond in any way, to swerve or to shield myself. And yet the events seemed to occur in
> 40   slow motion. As my bike slammed against the door I was

able to see that I was hitting it from the wrong direction: instead of pushing the door shut, I was pushing it further open. I felt it screech and bend but then stop as the momentum transferred itself from the door back to the bike
45 and especially to the most mobile part of the bike, which was me. I remembered that my feet were in the stirrups and if they remained fastened, I would get tangled in the bike and might break both my legs. But then, as if in answer, my feet detached themselves, like two peas popped from a pod, and
50 I flew over the door, leaving my bike behind.

 # Progress check

Now you have practised the skills needed for a Grade 5 response to Question 4. Use three different coloured pens to highlight passages of your answer to Activity 6 to show where you have satisfied each of the criteria for higher grades.

Then complete the progress check by checking relevant boxes below.

		Check ✓
Explaining how writers use structure to achieve effects and influence readers	I can evaluate *clearly* the effects on the reader.	
	I can show a *clear* understanding of the writer's methods.	
	I can make a *clear* and *relevant* response to the focus of the statement.	
Supporting your ideas with appropriate textual references	I can select a range of relevant textual references.	

Overview of the Writing section

What do you need to do?

The Writing section of Paper 1 is worth 40 marks, the same as the Reading section. You should expect to spend about 45 minutes on your writing, splitting this into three stages:

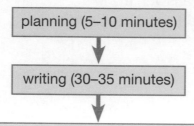

planning (5–10 minutes)

writing (30–35 minutes)

checking, proofreading and making final improvements (5 minutes).

You will be given a choice of two writing tasks. You must complete one of these tasks.

The exam paper will present you with a choice of one of the following combinations:

- a narrative task (story or series of events from your own or a character's experience) and a description task (describing a person, place or event)

- two narrative tasks

- two descriptive tasks

The tasks will be based on the theme of the text in the Reading section but you will not need to use any of the content from it. Your writing will be your own creation based on your imagination and life experiences.

How your writing will be marked

Your writing will be marked against two Assessment Objectives

Assessment Objective	The writing skills that you need to demonstrate
AO5 (Content and organization)	Communicate clearly, effectively and imaginatively, selecting and adapting tone, style and register for different forms, purposes and audiences. Organize information and ideas, using structural and grammatical features to support coherence and cohesion of texts.
AO6 (Technical accuracy)	Use a range of vocabulary and sentence structures for clarity, purpose and effect, with accurate spelling and punctuation.

The writing question in Paper 1 is worth a maximum of 40 marks:

- 24 marks are available for content and organization (AO5)
- 16 marks are available for technical accuracy (AO6).

What is content and organization?

To gain good marks for content and organization you need to:

- communicate your ideas clearly and effectively
- match your writing to whatever purpose, audience and form you have been given.

You will need to make deliberate choices of language and textual features, so that your writing has the intended impact on readers. To assess this, the examiner will look at:

- the way you use individual words and phrases
- the way you sequence, link and present your ideas
- the organization of your whole piece of writing, and the paragraphs and sections within it.

What is technical accuracy?

Technical accuracy is using words, punctuation and grammar correctly. Your written response needs to show that you can:

- use a range of vocabulary
- spell correctly, including more complex and sophisticated words
- write in correctly punctuated sentences
- use a variety of sentence forms to achieve specific effects
- write in Standard English.

Look back at your writing skills self-evaluation on pages 8–9 to remind yourself of the key skills to achieve your target grade in this section.

The descriptive task

What is description?

A description aims to paint a picture of a scene, person or experience in the reader's mind. It tends to focus on a moment in time, unlike a narrative which presents a changing series of events.

The descriptive task in Section B will provide a written prompt, scenario or visual image to act as a stimulus for your writing, so use this to help you to develop your ideas as you plan.

Look at the following example task.

Example Exam Question

You have been asked to write an entry for a creative writing competition.

Your entry will be judged by a panel of people of your own age.

Write a description suggested by this picture:

Planning your description

Vocabulary choices

When you write a powerful description of a place you need to help your reader imagine they are there. Think about how you can appeal to the reader's five senses to convey the sights, sounds, smells, tastes and physical experiences of the place you are describing. The vocabulary choices you make should help communicate the atmosphere of the place.

Look at the following notes a writer has made to help them describe a visit to a night market in Cambodia in South East Asia, where some unusual food is sold and eaten.

Place:	Night market in Cambodia
Sights:	tightly packed stalls, piles of shiny vegetables, trays of grasshoppers, baskets of ancient duck eggs, live crabs scuttling on the floor, sleepy children, mopeds weaving between stalls
Sounds:	whine of moped engines, hissing of the frying woks, excited conversations, stall-holders shouting, customers barking orders
Smells:	oil, frying, sweaty customers, spicy aromas
Tastes:	eating deep-fried tarantula – crunchy like hairy twiglets, sludgy
Sensations:	jostled by the crowd, overwhelmed by the choice, stomach rumbling
Atmosphere:	busy, breathless, rushing, excited

Activity 1

Using the prompts in the box, make some notes to help you plan your description as suggested by the picture on page 58. Try to choose words that will help the reader imagine the place.

Name of place: _____

Sights: _____

Sounds: _____

Smells: _____

Tastes: _____

Sensations: _____

Atmosphere: _____

Figurative language

Using figurative language such as **similes**, **metaphors** and **personification** can help a reader to imagine the place, person or experience you are describing. Thinking up effective examples at the planning stage can help you to remember to include these techniques when you write your description.

Look back at the notes about the Cambodian night market on page 59. Here the writer has included a simile to help describe the taste of eating a deep-fried tarantula:

crunchy like hairy twiglets

Activity 2

1. Look back at the notes you made to help you plan your description on page 59. Did you include any examples of similes, metaphors and personification?

2. Note down some examples of figurative language you could include in your description. Remember you want to create a sense of the place and atmosphere in the mind of the reader, so think carefully about the imagery you use.

Similes: _____

_____

_____

_____

Metaphors: _____

_____

_____

_____

Personification: _____

_____

_____

_____

Key terms

simile: a comparison showing the similarity between two quite different things, stating that one is like the other, for example, 'His hand was like ice'

metaphor: a comparison showing the similarity between two quite different things, where one is described as the other, for example, 'The sky was a glistening fabric full of sparkle and colour'

personification: giving human qualities or emotions to something non-human, for example, 'the flowers danced in the morning sunlight'

Exam tip

Do not use too many examples of figurative language. One or two effective examples will help your reader to imagine the scene you are describing. Too many can make it sound clumsy.

Narrative perspective

When you are writing a description, you must decide on the narrative perspective you are adopting.

You could choose to write in the:

- first person – presenting a single viewpoint from the perspective of the person writing the description, using personal pronouns 'I' or 'we'
- second person – presenting a single viewpoint as if from the reader's perspective, using the personal pronoun 'you'
- third person – presenting different people's viewpoints or the thoughts of a single person who is not the person writing the description, using personal pronouns such as 'he', 'she' or 'they'.

Activity 3

Read the extract below from a description of the food on display at the Cambodian night market.

> In a fug of alien noise and smells we pass neat pyramids of tiny glistening brains…

1. Tick whether the piece is written in first, second or third person.

   ☐ First person

   ☐ Second person

   ☐ Third person

2. Circle the word in the extract that establishes the narrative perspective.

Activity 4

Look again at the picture on page 58 and decide on the narrative perspective you will write your description from. For example, you could choose to write in the:

- first person from the perspective of a shopper
- first person from the perspective of a stall-holder
- third person from the perspective of an observer outside of the picture.

Tone and attitude

A writer's attitude towards the person, place or experience they are describing is revealed through *what* they choose to describe and the words they choose to describe them.

Activity 5

The writer describing a visit to a Cambodian night market has decided to write their description from a first-person narrative perspective, as a tourist visiting the market for the first time.

1. Look at the following extract about edible spiders for sale in the Cambodian market.

> When they arrive, the arachnids have been arranged as if they are chasing each other around the plate. Their legs crunch like hairy twiglets; their abdomens are full of nondescript bitter brown sludge. I can't imagine developing a taste for them.

2. Do you think the writer's attitude towards the food is positive or negative? Mark the attitude that they are conveying on the line below with an asterisk. One example has been done for you.

3. Pick out three examples of words or phrases that establish tone and convey the writer's attitude. Add these to the line.

4. Using details from this writer's notes on page 59, continue the following sentence using language to create a **tone** of disgust at the sights the writer sees.

In a fug of alien noise and smells we pass neat pyramids of tiny glistening brains...

_____

_____

_____

_____

_____

Key term

tone: manner of expression that shows the writer's attitude, for example, a humorous, sarcastic or angry tone

Activity 5 continued

5. Now continue the following sentence using language to create a tone of excitement at the sights the writer sees.

Nearby, a purple-edged crab scutters past my toes as it escapes from a bucket and makes a bid for freedom...

Activity 6

Look again at the picture on page 58.

1. What attitude do you want to present towards the place you are describing?

Attitude:

2. What tone do you want to create in your description?

Tone: (e.g. stressful, bored, excited)

3. Using details from your notes on page 59, write a short opening paragraph for your description of the place in the picture. Think carefully about the language choices you make to convey your chosen attitude and create an appropriate tone.

Structuring your description

As you plan your description, consider how you can guide your reader through the experience. What do you want to focus their attention on at the beginning of your description? How might this focus change as the description develops? The focus might change when there is:

- a change of location (for example, moving closer in to the scene or switching to another area such as from the kitchen to the eating area)

- a shift in time (for example, moving forward from day to night or from the past to the present)

- a shift in viewpoint (for example, cutting from one person's perspective to another's).

Read the paragraph below from the travel writing about the Cambodian market. Notice how the writer guides the reader through the scene, rather like a camera lens that moves across a market and focuses in on different images.

> Sleepy children sit atop piles of shiny vegetables while mopeds carve non-existent routes between tightly packed stalls. Trays of deep-fried grasshoppers are frozen in tableaux mid-leap. A man inspects a basket of black 'thousand-year' eggs: duck eggs that have been stored in ash and salt until the shells blacken, the whites turn to a brown fetid jelly and the yolks to a gentle green slime. Nearby, a purple-edged crab scutters past my toes as it escapes from a bucket and makes a bid for freedom, only to find itself square in a moped's path.

Activity 7

1. The paragraph contains four sentences. Each sentence focuses on a different subject in this busy scene. Complete the fourth subject in the box below:

   children   **grasshoppers**   **a man**   `_____`

2. Notice how the writer conveys the life of the market by linking each subject to an action. Complete the table below to identify the writer's techniques to convey the busy life of the market.

Subject	Verb	What the verb implies about the subject
1. Children	sit	they are still
2. Grasshoppers	are frozen	they are rigid and look strange
3. A man		
4.		

Now read Student A's paragraph about this marketplace, written from the viewpoint of a tourist.

> Discourse marker used to establish time and a change of place.

Student A

As soon as we leave the food area, my friend and fellow tourist, Katya, has disappeared off towards the glittering Cambodian fabrics displayed by a tiny, smiling local woman. The purple and golden silks catch the electric lights from the groaning generators that hide beneath the trestle tables. Her hand reaches out, drawn to touch their smoothness and the stall holder knows she can begin her sales talk. 'I can give you good price,' she smiles. She knows that these tourists will pay more for her gems than the locals.

Activity 8

1. Write a contrasting paragraph to move the description of the market to the early morning. Establish a change in time in your first sentence by using an appropriate discourse marker and describe a quieter and less colourful scene as the night shoppers have gone and the stallholders pack up.

----

2. Check your paragraph. Did you include:

   • a change in focus? • figurative language? • vocabulary for effect?

3. Look back at the notes you made in Activity 1 on page 59. Create a paragraph plan to show how you will structure your description of a market. You could set out your plan like the example below.

Arrival at market – overwhelming first impression	
Focus on butcher's stall – butcher calling – crowds listening	
Move along to fruit stall – describe range of fruits	
Clothes and fake designer labels	
Small child in the crowds – focus in	
Quiet drink in café outside market – relief	

Writing your response

Using a variety of sentence forms

To secure a Grade 5 you must demonstrate your ability to use a range of different sentence forms to achieve specific effects. For example, you can use short sentences to give emphasis or use longer sentences to extend ideas. Look at how this is achieved in the following extract from a description of the Cambodian night market.

> Compound sentence to contrast the still children with the moving mopeds.

> Short simple sentence to emphasize the strange sight of this unsual food.

> Simple clause to introduce the eggs, followed by a list of their features.

Sleepy children sit atop piles of shiny vegetables while mopeds carve non-existent routes between tightly packed stalls. Trays of deep-fried grasshoppers are frozen in tableaux mid-leap. A man inspects a basket of black 'thousand-year' eggs: duck eggs that have been stored in ash and salt until the shells blacken, the whites turn to a brown fetid jelly and the yolks to a gentle green slime. Nearby, a purple-edged crab scutters past my toes as it escapes from a bucket and makes a bid for freedom, only to find itself square in a moped's path.

Activity 9

Look back at the picture on page 58 and the plan you made in Activity 8. Now write the opening paragraph of your description of the street market.

Remember to:

- use a variety of sentence forms to control the pace of your description and create deliberate effects

- think about the vocabulary and linguistic devices you use to help the reader imagine the place you are describing.

Activity 10

Now continue and complete your description.

Once you have completed your work, proofread it for errors. Remind
yourself of the following key features of good descriptive writing and check
you have addressed a range of them:

- a consistent viewpoint established and maintained
- vocabulary used for effect and to create a specific tone
- figurative language used to convey a sense of place and atmosphere
- new paragraphs used to indicate a shift in focus
- variety of sentence forms used to achieve specific effects.

The narrative task

What is narrative?

A narrative is built from a series of events. It can be: true and based on your own experience, an invented story from your imagination and a combination of the two.

In your exam, narrative and descriptive tasks are assessed against the same criteria, but the examiner will look for the following important features in narrative writing:

a well-described setting	an engaging event which makes the reader want to read on	believable characters created and conveyed through: physical description, thoughts, actions and speech

You may be asked to write a whole short story or just a part, for example, the opening of a story or its ending. For both, the examiner will be looking for development of character and action.

Look at the following example writing tasks.

Example task A

Write the opening part of a story entitled 'Escape'.

Example task B

Describe a time when you felt the need to escape.

Example task C

Write the opening to a short story suggested by this picture.

Look back at your writing skills self-evaluation on pages 8–9 and tick the skills that you need to prioritize to achieve your target grade.

Planning your narrative

Remember the narrative task will provide a written prompt, scenario or visual image to act as a stimulus for your writing, so link your planned ideas to this.

Think about the important features of narrative writing: character, setting and events. You need to plan a narrative that introduces and develops these key features.

Activity 1

Look at the example plan Student A has produced below to help her to write a narrative in response to task A on the opposite page.

Using this approach, plan your ideas for task B. Look back at the picture to help you to think about the character, setting and events you could include in your narrative and note these down in the right-hand column below.

	Write the opening part of a story entitled 'Escape'.	Describe a time when you felt the need to escape.
Character(s)	Two teenage girls on a day out.	
Setting	At the seaside. It is isolated and a storm has begun.	
Event (problem or challenge)	They need somewhere to shelter.	
Event (attempt to resolve problem or challenge – might not succeed)	They find an old fishing hut but having settled themselves, they find the storm increases and the hut begins to disintegrate in the storm as the sea waters rise towards it.	
Event (climax or conclusion)	A fisherman in a boat rescues the girls.	

Exam tip

When you are planning the plot, remember that it does not need to be based on a major event. What will help you reach your target grade is how the characters respond to an event and the way you develop the action.

In the exam, you could also use a spider diagram to plan your ideas for the narrative task. Look at the spider diagram Student B has produced to help him plan his ideas for example task B.

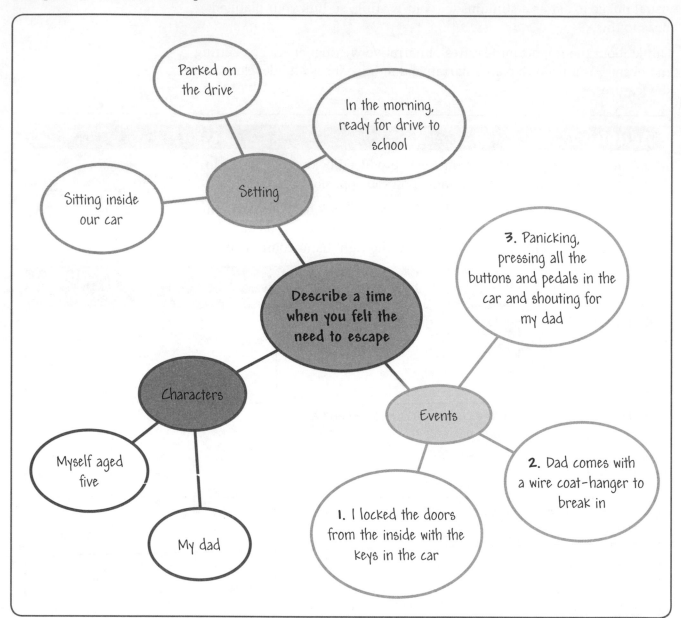

Activity 2

Use the spider diagram to plan your own response to example task B.

> **Describe a time when you felt the need to escape.**

You could base your plan on one of the following ideas or use your own:

- a time you went somewhere else to avoid a particular person
- a time when you were physically stuck somewhere
- a time when you wanted to escape from a situation or confrontation.

Activity 2 continued

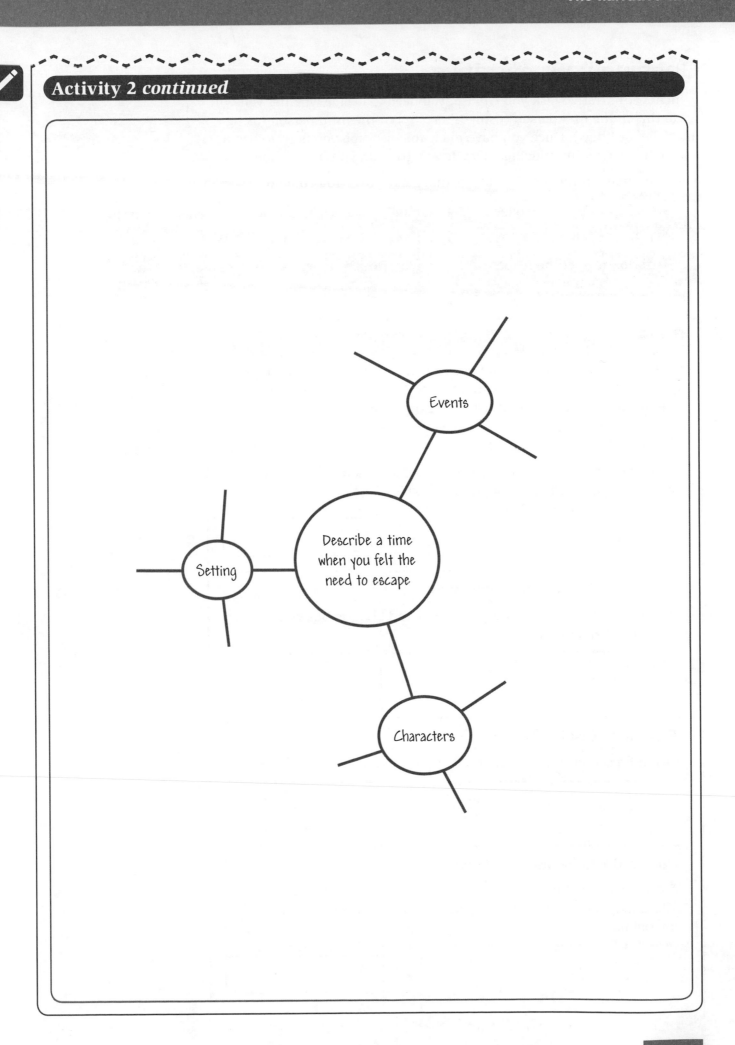

Opening your narrative

Whichever narrative task you choose, you need to decide whether you will write this in the first person (using 'I' or 'we') or the third person (using 'he', 'she' or 'they'). Once you have made this decision you need to begin your narrative by introducing characters, setting and an initial event.

There are many different ways of starting a narrative. You could use:

description – to introduce characters and/or the setting	**action** – begin with an exciting event, perhaps in the middle of the action
dialogue – let the reader hear the characters' voices	an **intriguing or unusual opening line** to capture the reader's interest

Activity 3

1. Read the following lines and decide which of the above techniques the author has used to start their story. Label each opening with 'description', 'action', 'dialogue' or 'intriguing'.

> ### *Demon Road* by Derek Landy
>
> Twelve hours before Amber Lamont's parents tried to kill her she was sitting between them in the principal's office…

> ### *Tanglewreck* by Jeanette Winterson
>
> At six forty-five one summer morning, a red London bus was crossing Waterloo bridge.

> ### *Exposure* by Kathy Reichs
>
> 'What I'd like from you is the truth, Miss Brennan.'

> ### *Double Cross* by Malorie Blackman
>
> The Glock 23 felt heavy and seductively comfortable in my hand. The pearl stock, warmed by my body heat, fitted snugly against my palm.

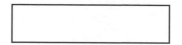

Activity 3 *continued*

2. Pick your favourite opening, the one that makes you to want to read more of the story. Explain the reasons for your choice.

Activity 4

Now look back at your plans for task B on pages 69 and 71 and choose which task you want to do. Write an opening paragraph that hooks the reader, using one of the techniques opposite.

Characterization, action and dialogue

To create a convincing and engaging narrative you need to develop your character or characters. You must show how they change and are changed by the action of your story.

Read the following extract from Stephen Fry's autobiography, *Moab is my Washpot*. Here, he remembers an event in his childhood when he was excited about having a perfect dead specimen of a mole, which he took into school for the nature table to show off to his class. As you read, think about how Stephen Fry shows how he was changed by the events of the narrative.

Moab is my Washpot by Stephen Fry

The next morning I bicycled down the mile-long lane to Cawston in a fever of excitement, the mole packed in straw in my saddlebag. This was to be my day of triumph.

'Here we have a common European mole,' I would tell the class. 'Pears *Family*
5   *Cyclopaedia* having been thoroughly exhausted on the subject of moles the night before. 'Moles eat their own weight every day and can actually starve to death within twelve hours if they don't have enough food. A mole is capable of burrowing up to eighteen feet in one hour. Thank you.'

I imagined executing a small bow and receiving delighted applause from all but a
10   frustrated, white-lipped Mary Hench, whose feeble puss-moth caterpillar or pathetic arrangement of barn owl pellets would go unnoticed.

I parked the bicycle and rushed to Miss Meddlar's slowing down as I arrived in the doorway, so as to look cool and casual.

'Well now, you're very early this morning, Stephen Fry.'

15   'Am I, Miss? Yes, Miss.'

'And what's that you have there? Something for the nature table?'

'Yes, Miss. It's a-' I started excitedly.

'Don't tell me now, child. Wait until class. Put it on the table … and well now whatever is going on?'

20   A violent explosion of giggles and screams could be heard coming from the playground. Miss Meddlar and I went to the window and tried to crane round and look towards the source of the uproar. Just then, Jimmy Speed, a chaotic, ink-stained boy, the kind that grins all the time as though he believes everyone to be quite mad, burst into the room.

25   'Oh, Miss, Miss. You'll never guess! You'll never ever guess!'

'Guess what Jimmy Speed?'

'That's Mary Hench, Miss! She's brought a donkey in for the nature table. A real live donkey! Come out and see. That's ever so beautiful, though how he will fit on the table I do not know.'

30   'A donkey!' Miss Keddlar went pink with excitement, straightened her skirt and headed for the door. 'A donkey. Good heavens!'

I looked down at my little mole and burst into tears.

Activity 5

1. Highlight the source text on the opposite page to identify how Stephen Fry as a writer shows his initial excitement in this passage. Use three different colours to identify:

   - words and phrases which describe his thoughts and feelings
   - words and phrases which describe his actions
   - dialogue which reveals his excitement.

2. Now identify the event that changes Stephen Fry's feelings in the text.

   _____
   _____

3. Explore how Stephen Fry as a writer introduces and develops this event. Using three different colours highlight:

   - different characters introduced to the story
   - dialogue used to show the impact of this event
   - words and phrases which show Stephen Fry's reaction to the event.

4. Write down what Stephen Fry's feelings are at the end of the passage.

   _____

Activity 6

Remind yourself of your chosen task and look back at your opening paragraph on page 73. Now write the next section of the narrative below, and continue on separate paper, developing the characters and action. Look back at your plan for this task and think about:

- how you can describe the event and show the impact it has
- how you can use dialogue and action to show characters' thoughts and feelings and the way these change.

Decide what kind of mood and atmosphere you want to create in your narrative. Think about how your vocabulary choices and the linguistic devices you use can help to create this.

   _____
   _____
   _____
   _____

Structuring your narrative

When developing your narrative, you need to use a variety of structural features effectively in order to gain your target grade. In the exam, you might see some of the following techniques:

- **shifts in time, location or focus** (for example, moving closer in to the action).

- **varying the narrative pace of the section**, that is, how quickly or slowly you take the reader through the action.

You have seen some examples of these structural features in the source texts you have read in the Paper 1 Reading section of this workbook. For example in the source text from 'The Birds' on pages 28–29, the writer structures the narrative using shifts in location, from the outside, to the bedroom, to the children's bedroom, as the birds move from the outside to the attack inside the house.

Exam tip

Remember these rules for dialogue for your own narrative:

- a new line for a new speaker
- punctuation inside the speech marks
- speech marks around the actual words spoken
- use of reporting verbs to show the speaker's tone or actions.

Activity 7

Study the visual image and then read the first section of Student A's narrative on page 77.

Activity 7 *continued*

Student A

The first time I saw the pair of blue patent shoes on a November Saturday, they sparkled at me. You may never know what it's like to have ridiculously narrow feet, but for me as a child, it meant one thing only … boring brown buckled shoes. Whichever shop we visited across London, this was the only footwear on offer for a child with feet as narrow as mine. And I could never be as fashionable as any of the other girls in my class.

So it was a month later, on Christmas day, that I approached the sqaure present under the tree, with the faint hope that perhaps, just perhaps, something blue might be underneath that paper.

1. Circle the words in the narrative that indicate the student structuring the writing using shifts in time.

2. Now write the next two paragraphs of the narrative, using shifts in focus as the narrator moves gradually nearer to the present and unwraps it. You should write on separate blank paper.

Activity 8

Now read another student's development of the narrative and highlight the discourse markers used to structure the writing. One has been done for you.

I walked slowly over to the tree, towards the box. I imagined my mother returning to that colourful window display one icy morning to make the purchase. I picked up the box in my hands and shook the package from side to side. I wondered if I could feel two items knocking against each other.

Eventually I began to open the parcel. First the bow and then the Sellotape. Everyone watched me, smiling. At last, I was in and able to see the top of the box. 'Nike' it said, with a big tick. The wait was over, but this was not what I had been waiting for.

Activity 9

Write the opening three paragraphs of a narrative in response to the following written prompt:

Write a story entitled 'Disappointment'.

You should use one or more of the structural features identified in the bullet-point list at the top of the opposite page. You could base your narrative on one of the following suggestions or use your own idea.

- a journey to an exciting event
- the giving/receiving of a gift
- meeting a hero
- a sports match
- moving to a new house
- making something that goes wrong

Write your answer on blank paper.

Exam tip

Remember that you need to start a new paragraph for:

- a change in topic
- a change of speaker
- a change of time
- a change of location.

Technical accuracy

In Section B you will be awarded up to 24 marks for AO5 (composition and organization) but do not forget that there are 16 marks available for AO6 (technical accuracy). To ensure that you gain as many AO6 marks as possible, make sure that you:

- re-read your writing as you go and leave enough time for a final proofread at the end
- remember to check that you have used a range of punctuation accurately
- use a range of vocabulary, including some sophisticated words
- write in full, accurate sentences
- use a range of sentence forms for effect
- check your spelling.

Activity 10

Remind yourself of your chosen task and look back at your opening paragraph on page 73 and how you developed the narrative on page 75. Use the following checklist to check the technical accuracy of your writing and make any necessary improvements.

1. **Vocabulary check**

   ☐ Check the vocabulary you have used. Underline any words that you consider to be sophisticated. These don't have to be long or complex, but they should be precise and well-chosen.

2. **Sentences check**

   ☐ Read through your writing again, focusing on sentence types. Do you vary your sentence lengths? Do you open your sentences in different ways? Does the pace of your writing change?

3. **Review**

   Make any changes that you think would improve the mark this response would receive for AO6. You might:

   - change some words to use more precise or sophisticated choices
   - replace two medium-length sentences with a short sentence followed by a longer one to create tension or to add detail
   - add paragraph breaks
   - edit any sentences that don't quite make sense.

45 minutes

Activity 11

Now that you have practised your descriptive and narrative writing skills, it is time to put them all together as you write a complete response to an example Paper 1 Section B writing task. Choose the form of writing that you find more difficult so that you can practise it.

You are going to write for the creative section of a general interest magazine aimed at people of your own age.

Either:

Write a description suggested by this picture:

Or:

Write a story about someone who faces a challenge.

Start your writing on page 80 and continue on blank paper.

Progress check

Now that you have practised the skills needed for a Grade 5 response to a Paper 1 Section B writing task, carry out the progress check below. Use three highlighter pens of different colours to highlight passages of your answer to Activity 11 on pages 77–78 to show where you have satisfied each of the criteria for a higher grade.

Basic skills descriptors	Check ✔	Target Grade 5 skills descriptor	Check ✔
I can show awareness of the intended audience of my writing.		I can consistently match the register I use in my writing to the audience I am writing for.	
I show simple awareness of the need to match my writing to purpose.		My writing is consistently matched to purpose.	
I use simple vocabulary and simple linguistic devices in my writing.		I can choose vocabulary for effect and use a range of linguistic devices to achieve effects.	
I use some relevant ideas in my writing and simply link these.		My writing is engaging, with a range of connected ideas.	
I try to use paragraphs, but my paragraphing is sometimes random.		I can use clear paragraphs and link them using discourse markers, although sometimes my paragraphing could be clearer.	
I can use some simple structural features in my writing.		I can usually use a variety of structural features effectively.	
I usually write in full sentences and can use full stops and capital letters accurately.		I can usually write in full and accurate sentences.	
I can use some punctuation marks, for example, question marks and speech marks.		I can usually use a range of punctuation.	
I try to use different sentence forms in my writing.		I can use a variety of sentence forms in my writing to achieve specific effects on the reader.	
I can use some Standard English and grammar, for example, agree verbs with their subject and maintain the tense of a written piece.		I can usually control my use of Standard English and grammar.	
I can spell basic words and some more complex words accurately.		I can generally spell correctly, including complex and irregular words.	
I can use a variety of vocabulary, including some complex words.		I can use a range of vocabulary, including some sophisticated words.	

Paper 2: Writers' viewpoints and perspectives

Overview of the exam paper

This exam lasts 1 hour 45 minutes and the exam paper is split into two sections.

Section A: Reading

- In this section you will read *two non-fiction texts*, one from the 19th century and one from either the 20th or 21st centuries. You must show your understanding of how writers from different time periods and genres present their ideas to influence the reader.

- You will have to answer four questions.

- This section is worth 40 marks.

Section B: Writing

- In this section you will write your own text to a specified audience, purpose and form in which you give your perspective on the theme that has been introduced in section A.

- This section is worth 40 marks.

How your reading will be marked

Below is a table that shows the Assessment Objectives (AOs) that you will be tested on in the Reading section of Paper 2.

Assessment Objective	The reading skills that you need to demonstrate
AO1	Identify and interpret explicit and implicit information and ideas. Select and synthesize evidence from different texts.
AO2	Explain, comment on and analyse how writers use language and structure to achieve effects and influence readers, using relevant subject terminology to support your views.
AO3	Compare writers' ideas and perspectives, as well as how these are conveyed, across two or more texts.

By working through the following chapter, you will practise these skills and learn exactly how and where to demonstrate them in the Paper 2 exam in order to achieve a Grade 5.

How your writing will be marked

Your writing will be marked against two Assessment Objectives:

Assessment Objective	The writing skills that you need to demonstrate
AO5 (Content and organization)	Communicate clearly, effectively and imaginatively, selecting and adapting tone, style and register for different forms, purposes and audiences. Organize information and ideas, using structural and grammatical features to support coherence and cohesion of texts.
AO6 (Technical accuracy)	Use a range of vocabulary and sentence structures for clarity, purpose and effect, with accurate spelling and punctuation.

The writing question in Paper 2 is worth a maximum of 40 marks:

- 20 marks are available for content and organization (AO5)
- 20 marks are available for technical accuracy (AO6).

What is content and organization?

To gain good marks for content and organization you need to:

- get your ideas across to the reader clearly
- match your writing to whatever purpose, audience and form you have been given.

You will need to make deliberate choices of language and textual features, so that your writing has the intended impact on readers. To assess this, the examiner will look at:

- the way you use individual words and phrases
- the way you sequence, link and present your points
- the organization of your whole piece of writing, and the paragraphs and sections within it.

What is technical accuracy?

Technical accuracy is using words, punctuation and grammar correctly. Your written response needs to show that you can:

- use a range of vocabulary
- spell correctly, including more complex and sophisticated words
- write in correctly punctuated sentences
- use a variety of sentence forms to achieve specific effects
- write in Standard English.

Question 1

Identifying explicit and implicit information and ideas

This question focuses on a set section of the source text. It tests your ability to identify:

- information and ideas that are **explicit**
- information and ideas that are **implicit**.

You will be asked to identify four true statements in a list of eight. Some of the statements that you will be given in this question must be inferred or deduced from the text. In order to work out whether they are true or not, you will need to read the text carefully and test each statement against your understanding of the information presented in the set section of the source text.

The following steps could help you to answer Question 1:

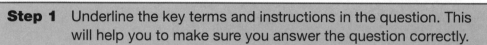

Step 1   Underline the key terms and instructions in the question. This will help you to make sure you answer the question correctly.

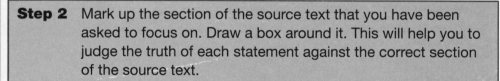

Step 2   Mark up the section of the source text that you have been asked to focus on. Draw a box around it. This will help you to judge the truth of each statement against the correct section of the source text.

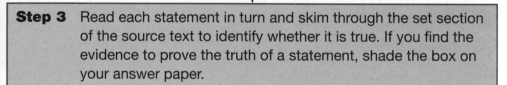

Step 3   Read each statement in turn and skim through the set section of the source text to identify whether it is true. If you find the evidence to prove the truth of a statement, shade the box on your answer paper.

Identifying implicit statements

An important feature of this question is that some statements are likely to contain information that is not stated directly in the text.

Read the brief extract below. In the exam, remember the skills you need to answer Question 1 are the same whether the text is from the 19th, 20th or 21st century.

> Joseph Merrick was born with severe deformities, which disfigured his body. This extract was first published in 1884.
>
> --
>
> **The Autobiography of Joseph Merrick** **by Joseph Merrick**
>
> I was sent about the town to see if I could procure work, but being lame and deformed no one would employ me; when I went home for my meals, my step-mother used to say I had not been to seek for work.

Activity 1

Look at the following four *true* statements about this extract.

    A   Merrick was told to find work. ☐

    B   Merrick's body was disabled. ☐

    C   Merrick's father had remarried. ☐

    D   Merrick's stepmother was unkind to him. ☐

1. Using one colour, highlight the two statements which are supported by explicit evidence from the text.

2. Using the same colour, underline the words or phrases from the text that support these statements.

One student has identified statement C as a true statement which is supported by explicit evidence from the text. Look at the word they have highlighted to support this statement.

> I was sent about the town to see if I could procure work, but being lame and deformed no one would employ me; when I went home for my meals, my step-mother used to say I had not been to seek for work.

From this word the student has identified implicit information that Merrick's father has remarried.

Activity 2

1. Using a different colour, shade another statement in Activity 1 which is supported by implicit evidence from the text.

2. Using the same colour, highlight the words or phrases from the text that support this statement.

Now read the following extract which is taken from *My Left Foot*, the autobiography of the Irish writer, Christy Brown, which was first published in 1954.

> Christy Brown was born with cerebral palsy, unable to control any part of his body except his left foot. His inability to speak effectively cut him off from his family. In this extract he describes his early childhood.
>
> ---
>
> ### *My Left Foot* by Christy Brown
>
> It was Mother who first saw that there was something wrong with me. I was about four months old at the time. She noticed that my head had a habit of falling backward whenever she tried to feed me. She attempted to correct this by placing her hand on the back of my neck to keep it steady. But
> 5   when she took it away, back it would drop again. That was the first warning sign. Then she became aware of other defects as I got older. She saw that my hands were clenched nearly all of the time and were inclined to twine behind my back; my mouth couldn't grasp the teat of the bottle because even at that early age my jaws would either lock together tightly, so that
> 10 it was impossible for her to open them, or they would suddenly become limp and fall loose, dragging my whole mouth to one side. At six months I could not sit up without having a mountain of pillows around me. At twelve months it was the same.
>
> Very worried by this, Mother told my father her fears, and they decided to
> 15 seek medical advice without any further delay. I was a little over a year old when they began to take me to hospitals and clinics, convinced that there was something definitely wrong with me, something which they could not understand or name, but which was very real and disturbing.

Activity 3

Look at the following statement:

A   Christy Brown's mother was observant.

1. Choose which *one* of the following pieces of evidence from the text prove this is a *true* statement. Circle your choice.

| 'It was Mother who first saw that there was something wrong with me.' | 'At six months I could not sit up without having a mountain of pillows around me.' | 'Mother told my father her fears, and they decided to seek medical advice without any further delay.' |

2. Write two more true statements about this text, based on lines 1 to 13. You could base these statements on the above pieces of evidence you didn't circle.

B _____

C _____

Read the newspaper article which begins below and then complete Activity 4 on page 88. The article is about shark-attack survivors campaigning for sharks' safety and was published in *The Guardian* newspaper on the 14 September 2010.

Source A

Shark attack survivors fight to save endangered species

Suzanne Goldenberg 14.9.2010

Nine victims want a ban on killing the fish
5 **just for the fins to make soup**

Thirty-five years after **Jaws** struck fear into cinema audiences, with the story of a man-eating great white, a group of shark attack victims has called on the UN to stop the world fishing sharks into extinction.

10 The nine victims want a ban on finning, a gruesome practice in which fishermen cut off a fin for shark fin soup and then dump the fish back in the water to drown or bleed to death. An estimated 73 million sharks are killed by finning each year. Nearly a third of all shark species are threatened or near threatened with extinction,
15 conservationists said.

For Krishna Thompson, a New York banker who nearly died after a shark took his left leg, the scale of that carnage easily trumps his personal loss. "I was attacked by a shark. Yes it was a tragedy but that is what sharks do, I can't blame the shark for what it did,"
20 he said. "You have to put that aside and look at the bigger picture: 73 million sharks killed yearly for shark finning." Yesterday's event, which was sponsored by the Pew Environment Group, was intended to put pressure on the United Nations to protect sharks.

Sharks, as top predators, are essential to the balance of the
25 marine environment. Remove sharks, and systems would collapse because of an abundance of smaller fish. But unlike other at-risk species such as tuna, there is no global management plan for shark fishing, said Matt Rand, director of global shark conservation for Pew.

30 "Right now in the open ocean there are no limits on the number of shark that can be caught," said Rand. "It is the wild west out there and that is not a sustainable situation." The cultural staying power of Jaws has not helped cultivate sympathy for the species either.

35 Thompson was on a trip to Bahamas to celebrate his 10th wedding anniversary in 2001 when he was attacked in about five feet of water. "I was treading water not too far out when from the corner of my eye I saw a dark fin approach me," he said.

Glossary

Jaws: a famous film from the 1970s about Great White Shark attacks

40 The shark swam between his legs before he heard it crunching into the bone of his left leg, and then shook his body violently as it tried to tow him out to sea. Thompson used both his hands to free his leg, and then beat the shark until it released him.

A doctor on the beach applied a makeshift **tourniquet**, and he was **medivaced** back to the US where his leg was later
45 amputated below the knee.

"If I could endure such an attack and lose a limb and still support shark conservation, I don't see why anybody else shouldn't," he said. "I don't even want to think about what the oceans would be like if we didn't have sharks. I know it wouldn't be good."

Glossary

tourniquet: tight bandage to stop bleeding

medivaced: evacuated for medical treatment

Activity 4

Read the article again, from lines 1 to 23.

Choose four statements below that are *true*.

- Shade the boxes of the ones that you think are true.

- Choose a maximum of four statements.

A	Finning is contributing to decreasing numbers of sharks.	☐
B	Not all shark species are at risk of extinction.	☐
C	The writer believes that finning is cruel.	☐
D	The writer is sympathetic to the fact that shark fishermen need to earn a living.	☐
E	The writer was attacked by a shark.	☐
F	Some people who have been attacked by sharks want to kill them.	☐
G	One victim, Thompson, believes that it is natural for sharks to attack people.	☐
H	A global fishing plan to limit shark fishing might improve the situation.	☐

Check your answer to Activity 4 on page 88 against the list of correct true statements given below.

A   Finning is contributing to dwindling numbers of sharks.

B   Not all shark species are at risk of extinction.

C   The writer believes that finning is cruel.

G   One victim, Thompson, believes that it is natural for sharks to attack people.

 # Progress check

Reflect on your answer to Activity 4 and use the following checklist to assess your progress.

	Yes	No
Did you read the statements very carefully to make sure that you understood them before you chose?		
Did you re-read the text to make sure that you had not misinterpreted it?		
Did you check that you had only chosen *four* statements?		
Would you have been awarded full marks for this question?		

Exam tip

When answering Question 1 in the exam, check whether any of the names mentioned in the statements refer to the writer of the text or to another person entirely.

Question 2

Synthesis and interpretation

This question assesses your ability to select information and ideas from two texts and **synthesize** them into a clear answer. To produce a Grade 5 response you will need to:

- make *clear **inferences*** from both texts
- select *clear references/textual details* relevant to the focus of the question
- make *statements that show clear differences* between texts.

Look at the example Question 2 below, then read Source A on pages 87–88 and Source B on the opposite page.

synthesize: to combine information and ideas from different texts

inference: an opinion drawn from what someone implies rather than from an explicit statement

Example Exam Question

2 You need to refer to Source A and Source B for this question:

Use details from both sources. Write a summary of the similarities in how sharks are regarded by people who use the sea.

Activity 1

1. Circle the key words in the question above.

2. Read Source A and Source B. Which aspects of sea-users' attitudes to sharks can you identify in *both* texts? Tick each relevant aspect below which is common to both texts. The first one is done for you.

   Aspects:

Swimmers' attitudes towards sharks ☑	Film-goers' attitudes towards sharks ☐
Fishermen's attitudes towards sharks ☐	The writer's attitudes towards sharks ☐
Government attitudes towards sharks ☐	

The aspects you choose can be a useful way of organizing your answer to Question 2. You could write one paragraph about each of the three strongest aspects you have identified to create a three-paragraph answer. In each paragraph you should:

- make a statement about a clear similarity or difference between the two texts

- select evidence from both texts relevant to the aspect you have identified

- make clear inferences from the references/textual details selected to support your statement.

Exam tip

When referring to each text in the exam, you might use the author's surnames, 'Source A' and 'Source B' as named in the exam paper, or journal versus newspaper article. Try to be consistent and don't waste time copying out long titles and author names.

This is an extract from a 19th-century travel journal. On a visit to Sydney in Australia, the American author Mark Twain describes the relationship between men and sharks in the harbour of the city.

Source B

'Following the Equator' by Mark Twain, 1897

And finally comes the shark-fishing. Sydney Harbour is **populous** with the finest breeds of man-eating sharks in the world. Some people make their living catching them; for the Government pays a cash **bounty** on them. The larger the shark the larger the bounty,
5   and some of the sharks are twenty feet long. You not only get the bounty, but everything that is in the shark belongs to you. Sometimes the contents are quite valuable.

The shark is the swiftest fish that swims. The speed of the fastest steamer afloat is poor compared to his. And he is a great **gad-**
10 **about**, and roams far and wide in the oceans, and visits the shores of all of them, ultimately, in the course of his restless excursions…

The people of Sydney ought to be afraid of the sharks, but for some reason they do not seem to be. On Saturdays the young
15 men go out in their boats, and sometimes the water is fairly covered with the little sails. A boat upsets now and then, by accident, a result of tumultuous **skylarking**; sometimes the boys upset their boat for fun—such as it is with sharks visibly waiting around for just such an occurrence. The young fellows scramble
20 aboard whole—sometimes—not always. Tragedies have happened more than once. While I was in Sydney it was reported that a boy fell out of a boat in the mouth of the Paramatta river and screamed for help and a boy jumped overboard from another boat to save him from the assembling sharks; but the sharks made swift work
25 with the lives of both.

The government pays a bounty for the shark; to get the bounty the fishermen bait the hook or the **seine** with agreeable **mutton**; the news spreads and the sharks come from all over the Pacific Ocean to get the free board. In time the shark culture will be one of the
30 most successful things in the colony.

Glossary

populous: crowded, full

bounty: reward

gad-about: traveller

skylarking: messing around

seine: fishing net

mutton: meat from a fully grown sheep

✏️ **Activity 2**

1. Choose the three strongest aspects you identified in Question 2 of Activity 1 and add these to the first column in the table below.

	Source A	Source B

2. Now add a clear statement about how each aspect is presented in each source text to the table.

Selecting clear and relevant textual details

When answering Question 2, it can be very easy to focus on one source text. You need to ensure you make clear references or select clear textual details from *both* texts to support your answer. Make sure you pick the most relevant references/textual details to make best use of exam time.

Statement 1

The writer thinks that sharks will do better than people: 'the shark culture will be one of the most successful things in the colony'.

Statement 2

The writer thinks the thriving sharks will become 'the most successful things' in Australia.

Activity 3

Read the statements and quotations about Source B below. Which quotation offers the best support to the statement made?

Statement: Fishermen are most interested in catching big sharks for profit

- 'The larger the shark the larger the bounty' ☐
- 'some of the sharks are twenty feet long' ☐
- 'Some people make their living catching them; for the Government pays a cash bounty on them'. ☐

Statement: Local people are relaxed about sharing the harbour with sharks

- 'The people of Sydney ought to be afraid of the sharks' ☐
- 'sometimes the boys upset their boat for fun' ☐
- 'he is a great gad-about' ☐

When answering Question 2 in the exam, you can use discourse markers to organize your answer and show the inferences, differences and similarities you have identified. Practise using the discourse markers in the table below.

Differences	Similarities	Inference
Although... Whereas... However... Unlike... On the other hand...	Similarly... In the same way...	We can assume that... This suggests... We sense that...

Activity 4

1. Re-read Source A on pages 87–88. Now look at how a student has used the table below to collect relevant textual details from both texts and make clear inferences from these. Complete the final two rows in the same way to cover the aspects you identified in Activity 2.

Sea users [Point/aspect]	What they do or say about sharks [Evidence]	What this implies about their attitudes [Explanation]
Swimmers' interest in swimming over safety	**Source A** 'I was treading water not too far out' **Source B** '...sometimes the boys upset their boat for fun—such as it is with sharks visibly waiting around for just such an occurrence'	Swimmers give more thought to fun and sport rather than the danger of sharks.
Swimmers' attitude to sharks	**Source A** 'I don't even want to think about what the oceans would be like if we didn't have sharks.' **Source B** 'The people of Sydney ought to be afraid of the sharks, but for some reason they do not seem to be.'	Swimmers seem to think of sharks as natural rather than dangerous.
Fishermen's - - - - - - - - - - - - - - - -	**Source A** - **Source B** -	- -
- - - - - - - - - - - - - - - -	**Source A** - **Source B** -	- -

2. Now choose *one* aspect and write a paragraph about this on separate paper. In your paragraph you should:

   - make a clear *statement* about the identified similarity between the source texts
   - integrate relevant *references/textual details* from both texts
   - make clear *inferences* from the selected evidence to support your statement.

Clear synthesis

In order to achieve a Grade 5 for Question 2 you must show a clear synthesis and interpretation of both texts with relevant evidence from both texts. To synthesize you need to:

- select and combine relevant information from both source texts

- make clear inferences that show your interpretation of the references/ textual details you have selected.

Activity 5

1. Read the extracts opposite from three students' responses to the example Question 2 on page 90. Use the criteria below to evaluate each response.

   - Highlight or underline where the different criteria are demonstrated in each response. Mark the relevant letters next to the evidence. You can use any more than once.

   - Rank the answers in order of quality: 1 for the strongest and 3 for the weakest. Write a paragraph to explain your reasons.

Criteria	What this means
A Statement identifies clear similarity between the texts	Focus on *links* between the texts rather than retelling the content
B Selects clear and relevant references/textual details from both texts	Be sure to select quotations from *each* text
C Makes clear inferences from both texts	Base your interpretation of the text on the evidence you identify
D Shows clear synthesis and interpretation of both, combining information to create a summary (synthesis)	Create a new text by combining points from both texts, together with your inferences

My ranking of the candidates is: **Student A** ☐   **Student B** ☐   **Student C** ☐

The reasons for candidate _____ being the strongest answer are

----

The weakest candidate is _____ because

----

2. Did you notice where one candidate found a similarity but then refined it to show how they were different? This is skilful analysis. Underline that example and circle the discourse marker used to establish difference.

Student A

Lots of people have attitudes to the sharks in the texts. Swimmers go into the sea and sometimes sharks attack them. Fishermen kill sharks and they feed them to keep up the numbers. Even though these texts are written in different times it shows that not much has changed. The man who had his leg bitten wants to support the sharks and help to keep them in the sea because they are endangered and are being killed by fishermen. This seems weird when he has been attacked.

Student B

Both texts show that fishermen and people relaxing on the sea have attitudes to sharks. Source 1 shows that swimmers know that sharks are in the sea, but they still go there. The man mentioned is relaxed about sharks being present in the sea even though he was attacked: 'you have to put that aside'. Although unlike the Australian locals, he does not suggest he would be returning to swim alongside them. Source 2 shows that the people play in waters where sharks are present, and even throw each other off boats and 'upset their boat for fun'. This suggests they have a relaxed attitude towards sharks.

The fishermen described in both texts have the same attitude to sharks. Source 1 says that they make money from the shark fins '73 million sharks'. Source 2 shows that this happened even years ago in Sydney and fishermen 'make their living' from killing sharks which suggests that they make quite a lot of profit if they can live by fishing them.

Student C

The texts show attitudes about sharks from people that use the sea. The fishermen want to kill them and they make money from it, 'fishermen cut off a fin for shark fin soup.'

People that use the sea for pleasure care about sharks even though some of them have been attacked by them. Their attitude is that they care about sharks and the fact that they are endangered which reflects their attitude. Source 1 says 'I can't blame the shark for what it did'.

Activity 6

Remind yourself of the example Question 2 below.

Example Exam Question

2 You need to refer to Source A and Source B for this question:

Use details from *both* sources. Write a summary of the similarities in how sharks are regarded by people who use the sea.

Using the notes you have made in the previous activities in this section, write your full answer to this question. Remember you need to show clear synthesis and interpretation of both texts by:

- selecting relevant references/textual details

- making clear inferences from these.

Before you begin to write, look back at the extract from the student response you identified as the best answer on page 95. Think about how you can follow this example to:

- make clear statements about the similarities between the source texts

- integrate relevant references/textual details from both texts

- make clear inferences from the selected evidence to support your statements.

Remember to use the discourse markers on page 92 to guide the examiner through your answer as you write this. Use the writing space below and continue on blank paper.

Exam tip

In the exam you may encounter a text about a topic or time that you know something about. Remember this is a test of reading skills, so only include information from the source texts, rather than your personal knowledge or opinions.

8 minutes

Activity 7

Example Exam Question

2 You need to refer to Source A and Source B on pages 98–100 for this question:

Use details from *both* sources. Write a summary of the differences in the writers' experiences of living with disability.

Source A

The following extract is taken from *My Left Foot*, the autobiography of the Irish writer, Christy Brown, which was first published in 1954. Christy Brown was born with cerebral palsy, unable to control any part of his body except his left foot. His inability to speak effectively cut him off from his family. In this extract he describes his early childhood.

My Left Foot by Christy Brown

It was Mother who first saw that there was something wrong with me. I was about four months old at the time. She noticed that my head had a habit of falling backward whenever she tried to feed me. She attempted to correct this by placing her hand on the back of my neck to keep it steady. But
5   when she took it away, back it would drop again. That was the first warning sign. Then she became aware of other defects as I got older. She saw that my hands were clenched nearly all of the time and were inclined to twine behind my back; my mouth couldn't grasp the teat of the bottle because even at that early age my jaws would either lock together tightly, so that
10   it was impossible for her to open them, or they would suddenly become limp and fall loose, dragging my whole mouth to one side. At six months I could not sit up without having a mountain of pillows around me. At twelve months it was the same.

Very worried by this, Mother told my father her fears, and they decided to
15   seek medical advice without any further delay. I was a little over a year old when they began to take me to hospitals and clinics, convinced that there was something definitely wrong with me, something which they could not understand or name, but which was very real and disturbing,

Almost every doctor who saw and examined me labelled me a very
20   interesting but also a hopeless case. Many told Mother very gently that I was mentally defective and would remain so. That was a hard blow to a young mother who had already reared five healthy children. The doctors were so very sure of themselves that Mother's faith in me seemed almost an impertinence. They assured her that nothing could be done for me.

25   She refused to accept this truth – the inevitable truth as it then seemed – that I was beyond cure, beyond saving, even beyond hope. She could not and would not believe that I was an imbecile, as the doctors told her. She had nothing in the world to go by, not a scrap of evidence to support her conviction that, though my body was crippled, my mind was not. In spite of
30   all the doctors and specialists told her, she would not agree. I don't believe she knew why, she just knew, without feeling the smallest shade of doubt.

Finding that the doctors could not help in any way beyond telling her not to place her trust in me, or, in other words, to forget I was a human creature, rather to regard me as just something to be fed and washed and then put
35   away again, Mother decided there and then to take matters into her own hands. I was her child, and therefore part of the family. No matter how dull and incapable I might grow up to be, she was determined to treat me on the same plane as the others.

The following extract is taken from the autobiography of Joseph Merrick, a man who was born with a condition, which disfigured his body. This extract was first published in a pamphlet in 1884, produced by the owners of the freak show where Merrick was put on display to the visiting public.

The Autobiography of Joseph Merrick by Joseph Merrick

I first saw the light on the 5th of August, 1860, I was born in Lee Street, Wharf Street, Leicester. The deformity which I am now exhibiting was caused by my mother being frightened by an Elephant; my mother was going along the street when a
5   procession of Animals were passing by, there was a terrible crush of people to see them, and unfortunately she was pushed under the Elephant's feet, which frightened her very much; this occurring during a time of pregnancy was the cause of my deformity.

The measurement around my head is 36 inches, there is a large
10   substance of flesh at the back as large as a breakfast cup, the other part in a manner of speaking is like hills and valleys, all lumped together, while the face is such a sight that no one could describe it. The right hand is almost the size and shape of an Elephant's foreleg, measuring 12 inches round the wrist
15   and 5 inches round one of the fingers; the other hand and arm is no larger than that of a girl ten years of age, although it is well proportioned. My feet and legs are covered with thick lumpy skin, also my body, like that of an Elephant, and almost the same colour, in fact, no one would believe until they saw it, that such a
20   thing could exist. It was not perceived much at birth, but began to develop itself when at the age of 5 years.

I went to school like other children until I was about 11 or 12 years of age, when the greatest misfortune of my life occurred, namely – the death of my mother, peace to her, she was a good mother
25   to me; after she died my father broke up his home and went to lodgings; unfortunately for me he married his landlady; henceforth I never had one moment's comfort, she having children of her own, and I not being so handsome as they, together with my deformity, she was the means of making my life a perfect misery; lame and
30   deformed as I was, I ran, or rather walked away from home two or three times, but suppose father had some spark of parental feeling left, so he induced me to return home again.

I was sent about the town to see if I could procure work, but being lame and deformed no one would employ me; when I went home
35   for my meals, my step-mother used to say I had not been to seek for work. I was taunted and sneered at so that I would not go home for my meals, and used to stay in the streets with an hungry belly rather than return for anything to eat, what few half-meals I did have, I was taunted with the remark –– "That's more than you
40   have earned." Being unable to get employment my father got me

a **pedlar's** license to **hawk** the town, but being deformed, people would not come to the door to buy my wares. In consequence of my ill luck my life was again made a misery to me, so that I again ran away and went hawking on my own account, but my deformity
45 had grown to such an extent, so that I could not move about the town without having a crowd of people gather around me. I then went into the **infirmary** at Leicester, where I remained for two or three years, when I had to undergo an operation on my face, having three or four ounces of flesh cut away; so thought I, I'll get
50 my living by being exhibited about the country.

In making my first appearance before the public, who have treated me well –– in fact I may say I am as comfortable now as I was uncomfortable before. I must now bid my kind readers adieu.

Glossary

pedlar: a person who sells things

hawk: to sell goods by calling out

infirmary: hospital

Progress check

1. Look back at your answer to Activity 7 and use the following checklist to assess your progress. You could annotate your answer to pick out the evidence that shows each skill.

		Yes	No
Identifying and interpreting explicit and implicit information and ideas	I can make statements that show clear similarities between the texts.		
	I can make clear inferences from both texts.		
Selecting and synthesizing evidence from different texts	I can demonstrate clear interpretations of both texts.		
Supporting your ideas with appropriate textual references	I can select *clear* references/textual details relevant to the focus of the question from both texts.		

2. Identify any improvements you would need to make to your original answer to achieve the Grade 5 standard. Rewrite your response opposite, highlighting the changes you have made.

Question 3

Understanding how a writer uses language

This question assesses your ability to analyse the effects of a writer's choices of language. To produce a Grade 5 response you need to show *clear understanding* of language by:

- *explaining clearly* the effects of the writer's choices of language
- selecting a range of *relevant* textual details
- making *clear and accurate* use of subject terminology.

The skills highlighted will distinguish a Grade 5 response from a weaker answer. You will explore exactly what each of these skills requires you to do when answering Question 3 as you work through this section.

In the exam, this question could relate to either Source A *or* Source B. When you answer this question, remember to read the source text closely, looking carefully for the following:

words and phrases chosen for effect

language features, for example, metaphor, simile, and so on

sentence forms and patterns

In your response, you will need to explain the effects of these words and phrases, language features, and sentence forms and patterns in relation to the focus of the question.

Activity 1

Look back at what you must do to achieve a Grade 5 response to Question 3. Tick the top four elements from the list below that *must* be included in a Grade 5 answer:

- ☐ Textual details, for example, quotations and examples
- ☐ Points about language that link to the exact focus of the question asked
- ☐ One quotation to support your answer
- ☐ Comments about the writer's life
- ☐ Language terminology, for example, noun, metaphor, short sentences
- ☐ Explanation of the effects of the language used
- ☐ Comments on the text's structure
- ☐ Comments about whether you like or dislike the text

Exam tip

Remember to read the set section of the source text carefully. Pay attention to every word, phrase, piece of punctuation and sentence structure. Think about how the language features you identify can help you to answer the question set.

Answering the question

In the exam, you are advised to spend 15 minutes at the start reading through the source text and the questions. This will leave you 1 hour and 30 minutes to write your answers to the reading questions in Section A and complete the writing task in Section B. To help organize your time, give yourself 1 minute per mark for each reading question, plus checking time. As Question 3 is worth 12 marks, this means you should spend approximately 12 minutes on your answer, plus checking time.

Look at the following example Question 3.

Example Exam Question

3 You now need to refer *only* to *Source B*, from lines 1 to 32. How does Merrick use language to make readers curious enough to want to see him?

Follow the steps below to make sure your answer to Question 3 can achieve a Grade 5.

Step 1
- Read the question and underline the key effect it is asking you to explain.
- Underline which source text the question is about and identify whether you should look at the whole of the text or just part of it.
- If the question asks you to refer to an extract from the source text, draw a box around this section of the source text.

Step 2 Read the set section carefully and underline:
- words and phrases chosen for effect
- language features, for example, metaphor, simile, and so on
- sentence forms and patterns, for example, complex sentences, and so on.

Only identify words and phrases, language features, and sentence forms and patterns that are relevant to the focus of the question.

Step 3 Write your answer to the question.
Include the textual details you have underlined in the source text and explain their effects in line with focus of the question.

Step 4 Check your answer.

0 minutes

15 minutes

The following extract is taken from the autobiography of Joseph Merrick, a man with a condition, which disfigured his body. This extract was first published in a pamphlet in 1884, produced by the owners of the freak show where Merrick was put on display to the visiting public.

The Autobiography of Joseph Merrick by Joseph Merrick

I first saw the light on the 5th of August, 1860, I was born in Lee Street, Wharf Street, Leicester. The deformity which I am now exhibiting was caused by my mother being frightened by an Elephant; my mother was going along the street when a procession
5 of Animals were passing by, there was a terrible crush of people to see them, and unfortunately she was pushed under the Elephant's feet, which frightened her very much; this occurring during a time of pregnancy was the cause of my deformity.

The measurement around my head is 36 inches, there is a large
10 substance of flesh at the back as large as a breakfast cup, the other part in a manner of speaking is like hills and valleys, all lumped together, while the face is such a sight that no one could describe it. The right hand is almost the size and shape of an Elephant's foreleg, measuring 12 inches round the wrist and 5
15 inches round one of the fingers; the other hand and arm is no larger than that of a girl ten years of age, although it is well proportioned. My feet and legs are covered with thick lumpy skin, also my body, like that of an Elephant, and almost the same colour, in fact, no one would believe until they saw it, that such a thing could exist. It was
20 not perceived much at birth, but began to develop itself when at the age of 5 years.

I went to school like other children until I was about 11 or 12 years of age, when the greatest misfortune of my life occurred, namely – the death of my mother, peace to her, she was a good mother
25 to me; after she died my father broke up his home and went to lodgings; unfortunately for me he married his landlady; henceforth I never had one moment's comfort, she having children of her own, and I not being so handsome as they, together with my deformity, she was the means of making my life a perfect misery; lame and
30 deformed as I was, I ran, or rather walked away from home two or three times, but suppose father had some spark of parental feeling left, so he induced me to return home again.

Student A has annotated the source text, selecting words and phrases, language features, and sentence forms and patterns.

Look at the annotations. Some explain the effects created but others just identify language features.

Emotive language, using adjective 'terrible' and collective noun 'crush' to describe the mother's suffering

Facts to inform the reader

Anecdote, highly unusual, to interest the reader

Semi-colons linking three long sentences, to show link between the disaster and his condition

Suggests disaster, people are interested in disaster stories

Indications of time emphasize the mother's suffering

Shocking noun, sounds like he will look monstrous

Simile

Adjectival phrase

Comparison, using exaggeration/ hyperbole

Simile

Emotive language, noun 'thing'

Use of semi-colons to join up lots of sentences listing the sequence of negative events

Exaggeration/ hyperbole

Figurative language

Subclause to requalify his actions

I first saw the light on the 5th of August, 1860, I was born in Lee Street, Wharf Street, Leicester. The deformity which I am now exhibiting was caused by my mother being frightened by an Elephant; my mother was going along the street when a procession of Animals were passing by, there was a terrible crush of people to see them, and unfortunately she was pushed under the Elephant's feet, which frightened her very much; this occurring during a time of pregnancy was the cause of my deformity.

The measurement around my head is 36 inches, there is a large substance of flesh at the back as large as a breakfast cup, the other part in a manner of speaking is like hills and valleys, all lumped together, while the face is such a sight that no one could describe it. The right hand is almost the size and shape of an Elephant's foreleg, measuring 12 inches round the wrist and 5 inches round one of the fingers; the other hand and arm is no larger than that of a girl ten years of age, although it is well proportioned. My feet and legs are covered with thick lumpy skin, also my body, like that of an Elephant, and almost the same colour, in fact, no one would believe until they saw it, that such a thing could exist. It was not perceived much at birth, but began to develop itself when at the age of 5 years.

I went to school like other children until I was about 11 or 12 years of age, when the greatest misfortune of my life occurred, namely – the death of my mother, peace to her, she was a good mother to me; after she died my father broke up his home and went to lodgings; unfortunately for me he married his landlady; henceforth I never had one moment's comfort, she having children of her own, and I not being so handsome as they, together with my deformity, she was the means of making my life a perfect misery; lame and deformed as I was, I ran, or rather walked away from home two or three times, but suppose father had some spark of parental feeling left, so he induced me to return home again.

Like Question 2 of Paper 1, you must explain the effect of the writer's choices of language in line with the focus you have been given. Every time you identify a relevant word, phrase, language feature, or sentence form or pattern, ask yourself the following questions:

- Why has the writer chosen this?

- What effect does this have on the reader in line with the question asked? (In this question, how would it make readers feel curious enough to want to pay to see Merrick? Why might you, as you read it, wish you could actually see what he looked like?)

Read the explanation Student A has written linked to their first annotation. They have used the **point–evidence–explanation** structure to organize this response.

Key terms

point: a statement that links to the question asked

evidence: quotation or direct reference to the text

explanation: explanation of the effect of specific language features

Point

Student A

Evidence

Source B uses several facts at beginning of the article. One example is 'I first saw the light on the 5th of August, 1860'. As well as giving information this makes Merrick seem just like everyone else, in having a birth day. This helps the reader to feel surprised and sorry for him when they read on and find out about his disabilities.

Explanation

Activity 2

1. Using the point–evidence–explanation structure, write a paragraph about the following textual detail and annotation.

Emotive language, adjective   Collective noun

'there was a terrible crush of people to see them, and unfortunately she was pushed under the Elephant's feet'

----

2. Now do the same for the rest of the annotations on separate paper. Explain the effects of the words and phrases, language features, sentence forms and patterns identified. Remember your explanations should focus on how these make readers curious enough to want to see Merrick.

Exam tip

In the exam, don't just concentrate on words and phrases. You should also explain how the writer uses language features and sentence forms and patterns.

Read the opening of Student B's answer focusing on the same section of text (lines 1–32). It has been annotated to show how it demonstrates features of a Grade 5 response.

Feature identified using correct terminology

Student B

Relevant textual detail

Examines effect

Explains effect using adjective 'terrible' and collective noun 'crush' to describe the mother's suffering

Clear explanation

Range of language features mentioned

Explains effect

At first Merrick uses factual information to engage the reader in a life that seems normal. 'I first saw the light of day on 5th August 1860.' His life seems ordinary and that makes the reader relate to him as a normal person. When they find out shocking things about his appearance later the reader wants to know more because the factual ordinary language in the beginning contrasts with what is to come.

He describes a disaster that happened to his mother describing a 'terrible crush of people'. The emotive adjective 'terrible' and the collective noun 'crush' make the readers sympathise with the mother. The adverb 'unfortunately' shows that it was a disaster and people like to read about disaster stories.

To convey the disaster he uses punctuation in paragraph one to join three sentences into a very long sentence, with semi-colons. This shows how the events happened one after the other and ended up with him being born disabled which makes the reader feel sorry for him.

Subject terminology used clearly and accurately

Exam tip

When answering Question 3 in the exam, think about the words and phrases you use to introduce each explanation. This clearly marks your awareness of the *effect* of language rather than just spotting features. Sentence starters you should learn include:

- This suggests...
- This emphasizes...
- This conveys...
- This implies...
- This affects the reader by...
- The effect of this is to...
- This encourages the reader to think/consider...
- This invites the reader to question/wonder/consider...

Activity 3

1. Think of two further points to add to Student B's answer. Develop them into paragraphs to continue this Grade 5 answer at the same standard.

Another technique that Merrick uses ... _____
_____
_____

In addition, he uses ... _____
_____
_____

Clear and accurate subject terminology

In order to achieve a Grade 5 for Question 3, you need to make clear and accurate use of subject terminology in your response. Think about the focus of the question and link the references you make to different language features to the effects these create.

Activity 4

Look at the following examples of subject terminology you might have identified in Source B on page 104.

Choose the most relevant textual detail that demonstrates each feature and write a sentence to explain the effect it creates. The first one has been done for you.

- **Similes** to describe his appearance

Merrick uses a simile to help the reader imagine what his body looks like. The simile 'flesh at the back as large as a breakfast cup' might make the reader feel disgusted. Cups are normally something that you drink from but the description makes the reader imagine a cup made of fat flesh. Feeling disgusted, they would want to see Merrick with their own eyes and not just read about it.

- Adjectives to describe his features

- **Hyperbole** to emphasize how tragic some of his experiences felt

Key terms

simile: a comparison showing the similarity between two quite different things, stating that one is like the other, for example, 'His hand was like ice'

hyperbole: a deliberately exaggerated statement that is not meant to be taken literally

Activity 5

Look again at an example of Question 3.

Example Exam Question

> **3** You now need to refer *only* to Source A, Christy Brown's description of others' attitudes towards him (from lines 3 to 18).
>
> How does Brown use language to show how he feels about his mother?

1. Underline the key words in the question.

2. Read the set section from Source A below. As you read, annotate the text to identify relevant words and phrases, language features, and sentence forms and patterns that will help you to answer the question.

3. Add the relevant subject terminology to identify any features you identify.

Source A

The following extract is taken from *My Left Foot*, the autobiography of the Irish writer, Christy Brown, which was first published in 1954. Christy Brown was born with cerebral palsy, unable to control any part of his body except his left foot. In this extract he describes his early childhood.

- -

My Left Foot by Christy Brown

Almost every doctor who saw and examined me labelled me a very interesting but also a hopeless case. Many told Mother very gently that I was mentally defective and would remain so. That was a hard blow to a young mother who had already reared five healthy children.

5 The doctors were so very sure of themselves that Mother's faith in me seemed almost an **impertinence**. They assured her that nothing could be done for me.

She refused to accept this truth – the **inevitable** truth as it then seemed – that I was beyond cure, beyond saving, even beyond hope.

10 She could not and would not believe that I was an imbecile, as the doctors told her. She had nothing in the world to go by, not a scrap of evidence to support her conviction that, though my body was crippled, my mind was not. In spite of all the doctors and specialists told her, she would not agree. I don't believe she knew why, she just knew,

15 without feeling the smallest shade of doubt.

Finding that the doctors could not help in any way beyond telling her not to place her trust in me, or, in other words, to forget I was a human creature, rather to regard me as just something to be fed and washed and then put away again, Mother decided there and then to take

20 matters into her own hands. I was her child, and therefore part of the family. No matter how dull and incapable I might grow up to be, she was determined to treat me on the same plane as the others.

Glossary

impertinence: rudeness

inevitable: impossible to avoid

Activity 6

Write your answer to the example Question 3 on page 109, focusing on the extract by Christy Brown and remembering to use the point–evidence–explanation writing structure for analysis. Remember, to produce a grade 5 response you will need to:

- *explain clearly* the effects of the writer's choices of language
- select a range of *relevant* textual details
- make *clear and accurate* use of subject terminology.

The following extract is taken from the book *Dear Me: A Letter to My Sixteen-Year-Old Self*, which was first published in 2009. In this letter, the adult author, Fay Weldon, offers advice to her teenage self. Read the extract and complete Activity 7 on page 112.

complete Activity 7 on page 112.

Source A

Dear Faye, back then –

Stop worrying. There is nothing wrong with you. Your family is totally nuts but you are perfectly sane. You are living with your mother and your sister in one room in North London, and have had to spend the day in bed to keep warm, the year being
5   1947 and this being the famous freeze. You've come from New Zealand, the land of plenty, to this grey grisly city only months after World War II ended, and if you feel a little confused it is not surprising. You may also be feeling hungry too. There's whale meat for dinner and the butter ration is less than 50 grams a week. Get used to it. You're going to be on one diet or another for the rest of your life anyway. There'll even
10 come a time when you'll eat nothing but cabbage for days of your own free will. And by the way if you go up the road to Belsize Park Underground Station (slogan on the posters: It's Warmer Underground) and stand in the doorway – they won't let you in without a ticket – a blast of hot air comes out every two minutes as a train passes through. Join the little clutch of excluded shiverers standing outside: it's friendly and
15 companionable. Smokers today have the same experience.

You've no mirror other than the tiny one above the basin in the communal bathroom, but I promise you, you don't look too bad. A bit stunned, probably. And not as good as your big sister but things will get better. Everything is going to get better. You're going to get a scholarship to a good school. And your mother is going to get a job as
20 a live-in cook/housekeeper and there'll be three rooms instead of one even if you do have to share it with a rat. And University is free and they'll even give you money to live on while you're there. It feels like wealth. And never coming first in class, but only ever second or third, doesn't mean you're stupid just that there's always someone in the world cleverer than you are. Learn this. And you will always have really good
25 friends. Enjoy them.

No use telling you to try and marry a banker because that's not your style – your style is **bohemian**: folk singers, artists, poets. Face it. And no, it's not that your legs are unusually short, just that your sister's are longer. And by the way, it's all very well to want to be loved for your mind alone, but your habit of dressing like **Miss Phoebe**
30 in the school production of J M Barrie's Quality Street when you were fourteen [...] buttoned up at the neck and wrists, will do you no favours. There's a lot to be said for showing a bit more flesh. Since you have it, flaunt it.

Blessings – and remember to send messages back to yourself in the past, like this one now –

35 Faye in the future

Glossary

bohemian: artistic and unconventional person

Miss Phoebe: a schoolmistress character in a play
   by the author J M Barrie, first performed in 1902

15 minutes

Activity 7

Example Exam Question

3 You now need to refer *only* to Source A, Weldon's letter from the beginning to line 15.

How does Weldon use language to convey advice to her teenage self?

Progress check

Look back at your answer to Activity 7 and use the following checklist to assess your progress. You could annotate your answer to pick out the evidence that shows each skill.

		Check ✔
Analysing how writers use language to achieve effects and influence readers	I can show *awareness* of language when I offer *simple comments* on the effects of language.	
	I can show *clear* understanding when I *explain clearly* the effects of the writer's choices of language.	
Using relevant subject terminology to support your views	I can make *simple use* of subject terminology when writing about language.	
	I can use subject terminology *clearly and accurately* when writing about language.	
Supporting your ideas with appropriate textual references	I can select *simple references or textual details.*	
	I can select a *range of relevant textual details*.	

Question 4

Comparing writers' ideas and perspectives

Question 4 assesses your ability to compare the whole of both texts, focusing on the writers' ideas and perspectives and how they are conveyed. To produce a Grade 5 response you will need to:

- compare ideas and perspectives in *a clear and relevant way*
- *explain clearly* how writers' methods are used
- select *relevant supporting detail* from both texts
- show a *clear understanding* of the different ideas and perspectives in both sources.

You will now explore each of these key skills in turn to help you to build and develop the skills you need to produce a Grade 5 response to Question 4.

This question is worth 16 marks (a high proportion of the marks on this paper) so you should spend 20 minutes on it. It brings together all the skills you have used to answer the earlier questions. Now combine these skills to compare two texts from different centuries.

Activity 1

Question 4 might ask you to compare how writers convey their:

- ideas or attitudes
- viewpoints or perspectives
- experiences.

Draw a line to match each word or phrase in the left-hand column to its definition in the right-hand column. Remember to think about what each phrase means in the context of answering Question 4.

Question focus	Definition
Writer's ideas or attitudes	A point of view on a particular topic, for example, in support of, against
Writer's viewpoint or perspective	Things that have happened to the writer that might affect, teach or change their attitudes
Writer's experience	Specific thoughts and suggestions a writer considers about a topic

Identifying writers' ideas and perspectives

When answering Question 4 in the exam, you need to make sure that you can identify and understand:

- the *perspective* of each writer: when they are writing and what values do they hold

- the *context* in which they are writing: when the text was published and how that might shape their perspective.

Then you must consider how the writer conveys their ideas and perspectives. A key criterion for Question 4 is to explain clearly how writers' methods are used.

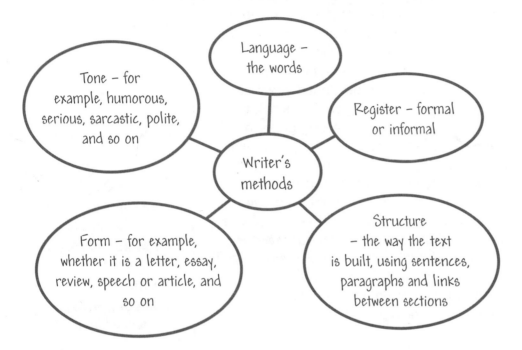

For example, read the source text on page 116. This is taken from *Shooting in the Himalayas*, a journal of sporting adventures and travel by Frederick Markham which was first published in 1854. This extract, written by a privileged military man, records shooting for sport during his travels in India. At the end of the 19th century, many people considered tiger hunting to be a noble sport linked to wealth, machismo and status.

As you read, ask yourself the following questions about the text:

- What is the opinion expressed about hunting?
- How has the writer chosen to convey his view about hunting?
  - How does the writer structure the writing to achieve this?
  - What language does the writer choose to achieve this?
  - How does the tone of the writing reflect this?

Source A

***Shooting in the Himalayas – a journal of sporting adventures and travel* by Frederick Markham**

Carefully we beat a most likely jungle, full of deer, peafowl, partridges **and c.**; not a shot was fired, lest the nobler game should be disturbed. At last, despairing of a tiger, we blazed away at everything, and had **capital** shooting until **tiffin** re-assembled
5 the party; one of whom, to our great distress, was brought in with his hand dreadfully shattered by the bursting of his gun.

Having sent him home under charge of Doctor Bruce, one of the party, who kindly went with him, and being satisfied he would be well taken care of, we beat steadily on, when three shots in quick
10 succession were fired on the right of the line – "Dekho sahib, dekho, bah!" screeched out by a dozen voices, sent the whole line in pursuit; the elephants, urged to their utmost speed, crashed through the jungle, screaming and trumpeting as they smelt the tiger; a waving line is seen on the surface of the long grass, as of
15 some large animal moving swiftly and stealthily along, and then, charging at full speed, the tiger with a final spring fixed himself upon Mayne's elephant, which, after a violent struggle, succeeded in shaking him off. Severely wounded, he retired into some long grass, and in making a second charge, was shot dead. He was a
20 fine animal, well grown, and full of pluck, and with our **maiden essay** in tiger shooting (for as a matter of course everybody killed him) we returned to camp, now pitched at Khanserai-chokee where we found our wounded man doing well, and able to bear being sent into the station during the night.

Glossary

and c: another way of saying 'etc.'.

capital: top quality, the best

tiffin: lunch

maiden essay: first attempt

Activity 2

What is the opinion about hunting expressed in Source A? Write down your ideas below.

Selecting relevant detail

Activity 3

1. The following student has identified that Markham and his companions are frustrated about their experiences at the beginning of the hunt. One textual detail to support this view is noted in the table below. Find another two textual details to support this and write these down in the table.

Markham's perspective	Evidence
At the beginning, he (and his guides) are frustrated	• 'Despairing of a tiger' • _____ _____ • _____ _____

2. Now re-read the text from where the tiger appears. Complete the table below to add one or two further points in the left-hand column about how Markham views the chasing and killing of the tiger.

3. Now add two examples of relevant textual details for each point.

Markham's perspective	Evidence
Hunting is exciting.	• _____ • _____
Hunting is pleasurable and a shared group experience.	• _____ • _____
Hunting is manly and involves human strength.	• _____ • _____
	• _____ • _____
	• _____ • _____

Now read an opinion column from *The Guardian* newspaper, which was published in 2015. In this column, the writer comments on the killing of Cecil the lion. This lion lived in the Hwange National Park in Zimbabwe and was wounded by an arrow shot by Walter Palmer, an American dentist and recreational big-game hunter.

As you read, ask yourself the following questions about the text:

- What is the opinion expressed about hunting?

- How has the writer chosen to convey her view about hunting?

  - How does the writer structure the writing to achieve this?
  - What language does the writer choose to achieve this?
  - How does the tone of the writing reflect this?

The first paragraph of the text has been annotated with some comments in response to these questions to support your thinking.

Source B

The hunter who killed Cecil the lion doesn't deserve our empathy

Trophy hunters like Walter J Palmer shouldn't receive death threats – but there is no excuse for their argument that hunting serves conservation

By Rose George 29th July 2015

> *Friendly and intimate tone with a rhetorical question to engage the reader.*

We love a good fight, don't we? Enter Walter J Palmer, a tanned dentist from Minnesota, with a bow and arrow. Along comes Cecil the lion, the alpha male of his pride, minding his own business being the best-known and most beloved lion in Zimbabwe if not
5   in Africa, as well as the subject of an Oxford University study. Then Cecil is shot with a bow and arrow, taking 40 hours to die, all because Palmer thought killing a magnificent animal was sporty.

> *Description of the first character seems comic.*

> *Description of the lion is heroic.*

> *Structure of the paragraph builds up to a shocking last line.*

I read the story of Cecil's killing and my education and intellect deserted me for a minute. I felt only disgust and rage, somewhat
10   inarticulately. I feel no calmness about big-game hunters. I am not persuaded by their justifications, which can be easily punctured with buckshot. Trophy hunting contributes to conservation, they say: when the Dallas Safari Club auctioned the right to kill an endangered Namibian black rhino, it said the $350,000 winning
15   bounty – they called it a "bid" – went towards conservation efforts in Namibia. There are only 5,000 black rhinos left.

The population of African lions has been reduced by 50% in the last three decades, says the International Fund for Animal Welfare, and there are now only 32,000. Elephants, leopards, polar bears
20   and giraffes are all hunted for "sport" too. Shooting an endangered species and calling it sustainable is like waving a fan and thinking you're helping to stop global warming.

In April, after Ricky Gervais tweeted a picture of the blonde, pretty Rebecca Francis lying next to a dead giraffe she had just shot, the

25　internet went ape. Arguably, it went more ape than it would have if she hadn't been female, and you can find plenty of earnest essays about how women have the right to be big-game hunters without getting an online hounding. I don't care what gender she was. I care that afterwards, she declared that she had done a good thing.

30　The giraffe was elderly, she wrote, and was going to die soon. By shooting him, she had honoured his life by making his body useful to locals: his tail could make jewellery and his bones could make "other things". "I'm no game biologist," she wrote, but "there is no question that hunters contribute the most to the welfare of

35　wildlife."

Follow this argument further and you reach the reasoning that poaching and trafficking do more harm than big-game hunting. True. Wildlife trafficking is worth $7-10bn, and is the fifth most profitable illegal market worldwide. Yet in many countries where

40　poaching is rampant, policing is patchy and punishment often nothing more than a fine. Yes, poaching is more damaging than trophy hunting. Murder is worse than grievous bodily harm, technically, but I'm comfortable strongly objecting to both.

But violently objecting to hunters can be almost as bad as

45　hunting. Most public displays of big-game hunting attract fury and sometimes death threats, as Palmer has been subjected to since his identity was revealed. The fact that African countries such as Namibia and Zimbabwe sell licences to shoot their own big game gets less attention.

50　Palmer is said to be "quite upset," but only because he got the wrong lion. He blamed his guides for this, rather than his own bizarre and repellent desire to augment his own self-worth (somewhat damaged, now, by a campaign to shut down his dental practice) by killing another creature.

55　Let's not turn Palmer and Francis into trophies too, repugnant though their actions are. I don't want to understand them or empathise. I'd rather not attempt to comprehend the inexplicable act that is the murder of animals for fun. But trophy hunting is about something bigger than that: an assumption that all animals

60　are at our service, and ignoring the fact that we are just clever animals too.

Here is a product of my superior animal brain: a plan. If you're going to pay $50,000 towards conservation efforts by shooting a lion, then give the money and don't shoot. Preserving life, by killing

65　fewer animals – now that would be worth a trophy.

Activity 4

What is the opinion about hunting expressed in Source B? Write down your ideas below.

Before you begin to answer Question 4 in the exam, it can be helpful to identify the text type, audience, purpose and source of each text. You can use the acronym 'TAPS' to help you remember this:

Text type: for example, a letter, speech, magazine or newspaper article

Audience: the intended reader or audience, for example, modern parents, educated adults in the late 19th-century or today's teenagers

Purpose: for example, to inform, persuade, argue, entertain, or a combination of these purposes

Source: where has the writing been taken from? When was it published? Does this tell you anything about the audience?

Activity 5

Identify the text type, audience, purpose and source of Source B on pages 118–119.

Text type: _____

Audience: _____

Purpose: _____

Source: _____

The writer of Source B includes a number of references to different people to support her opinion. With such a text you should establish clear understanding of who the writer is referring to.

Exam tip

Remember, in a text with a number of references, you must establish clear understanding of 'who is who' before you answer any exam questions.

Activity 6

Annotate Source B to establish who the people referred to are and, briefly, what you learn about them.

- Cecil the lion
- Walter J Palmer
- Rebecca Francis
- Ricky Gervais
- Rose George

Comparing ideas and perspectives

Look at the following example Question 4.

Example Exam Question

4 For this question, you need to refer to the *whole of Source A* together with the *whole of Source B*.

Compare how the writers convey their different views on hunting.

In your answer, you could:

- compare their different views and perspectives
- compare the methods they use to convey those views and experiences
- support your ideas with quotations from both texts.

Exam tip

Remember that in your final exam you will not have the time to make such detailed annotations as those below, but you might find it helpful to underline key quotations and add single word annotations to identify writers' methods.

Think about the similarities and differences between the views expressed by the authors of Source A and Source B towards hunting big cats. Rose George strengthens her argument by acknowledging some of the points made in support of hunting, but she immediately dismisses them.

Activity 7

Look at the annotations below by a Grade 5 student to identify the view conveyed about hunting at the end of Source B.

> She hates the actions of hunters.

> Animals are not for the pleasure of humans.

Let's not turn Palmer and Francis into trophies too, repugnant though their actions are. I don't want to understand them or empathise. I'd rather not attempt to comprehend the inexplicable act that is the murder of animals for fun. But trophy hunting is about something bigger than that: an assumption that all animals are at our service, and ignoring the fact that we are just clever animals too.

> She doesn't want to understand or share perspective.

> We are the same as animals.

Follow this model to complete your own annotations of both texts in line with the example Question 4. You could use the questions below to guide the annotations you make:

- What is the opinion expressed about hunting?
- How has the writer chosen to convey their view about hunting?
  - How does the writer structure the writing to achieve this?
  - What language does the writer choose to achieve this?
  - How does the tone of the writing reflect this?

Activity 8

Using the annotations you made in Activity 5, complete the table below to identify and compare the writers' different views on hunting and the details that suggest these. The left-hand column of the table suggests how you could structure your answer to the question.

Structure of your answer	Source A _ _ _ _ _ _ _ _ _ _ _ _ _ _ _ _	Source B _ _ _ _ _ _ _ _ _ _ _ _ _ _ _
Paragraph 1 of your answer	**Point:** hunting for sport can be frustrating and unfulfilling when you don't find your prey. **Detail:** 'despairing of a tiger we blazed away at everything'	**Point:** Some people think that hunting gives them glory. **Detail:** 'his own bizarre and repellent desire to augment his own self-worth… by killing another creature.'
Paragraph 2 of your answer	**Point:** **Detail:**	**Point:** Hunting cannot be regarded as a sport **Detail:** 'all because Palmer thought killing a magnificent animal was sporty'
Paragraph 3 of your answer	**Point:** Hunting provides honour and male bonding **Detail:**	**Point:** **Detail:**
Paragraph 4 of your answer	**Point:** **Detail:**	**Point:** **Detail:**
Paragraph 5 of your answer	**Point:** **Detail:**	**Point:** **Detail:**

Remind yourself of the example Question 4.

Example Exam Question

4 For this question, you need to refer to the *whole of Source A* together with the *whole of Source B*

Compare how the writers convey their different views on hunting.

In your answer, you could:

- compare their different views and perspectives
- compare the methods they use to convey those views and experiences
- support your ideas with quotations from both texts.

Look at the opening paragraph of Student A's answer to this question.

Student A

Both texts consider hunting as being a pleasure for leisure and sport. Source A describes the hunt as exciting and the shooting of the guns as 'capital shooting'. The word 'capital' suggests he thinks it is fun and exciting. In Source B the author takes the opposite view and believes that hunting should not be a pleasurable thing even though the dentist thought of hunting as sport. She says: 'all because Palmer thought killing a magnificent animal was sporty'. The word 'thought' suggests that the writer does not agree with Palmer.

Activity 9

Look back at the table you completed in Activity 8. Take one point and supporting detail about Markham's view from the Source A column and compare it with a contrasting point about George's view from your Source B column. Write a sentence to compare them, using the word 'whereas' to indicate the contrast.

In your answer to Question 4 you need to explain clearly how writers' methods are used. Look at the list of methods Student B has identified below, focusing on methods that are used in clearly similar or different ways in both texts.

> **Writers' methods**
>
> Emotional tone – indignant/glorifying
>
> Contrasting focus in consecutive paragraphs to structure the text
>
> Use of second-person pronoun
>
> Adjectives to describe
>
> Proper nouns of relevant people

Key term

tone: manner of expression that shows the writer's attitude, for example, a humorous, sarcastic or angry tone

In order to achieve a Grade 5 response to Question 4, you need to show a clear understanding of the different ideas and perspectives in both texts. It is not enough to simply state that the writer of Source A regards hunting as glorious whereas the writer of Source B describes it as selfish. You must go on to compare those views and explain clearly *the methods* used to convey them.

Activity 10

Re-read Source A and Source B. As you do so, ask yourself again the following questions about each text:

- What is the opinion expressed about hunting?

- How has the writer chosen to convey their view about hunting?

  - How does the writer structure the writing to achieve this?

  - What language does the writer choose to achieve this?

  - How does the **tone** of the writing reflect this?

Collect your ideas about the different methods each writer uses to convey their view in the following table:

Methods	Markham's view: He thinks hunting is exciting and glorious	George's view: She thinks of hunting as cruel and unjustifiable
Structure		
Language		
Tone		

Now look at a short extract from Student A's answer below to the example Question 4.

4 For this question, you need to refer to the *whole of Source A* together with the *whole of Source B*.

Compare how the writers convey their different views on hunting big cats.

In your answer, you could:

- compare their different views and perspectives
- compare the methods they use to convey those views and experiences
- support your ideas with quotations from both texts.

Look closely at the annotations which indicate where the answer displays features of a Grade 5 response. These annotations indicate where the answer:

- compares ideas and perspectives in *a clear and relevant way*
- *explains clearly* how writers' methods are used
- selects *relevant detail* to support from both texts
- shows a *clear understanding* of the different ideas and perspectives in both sources.

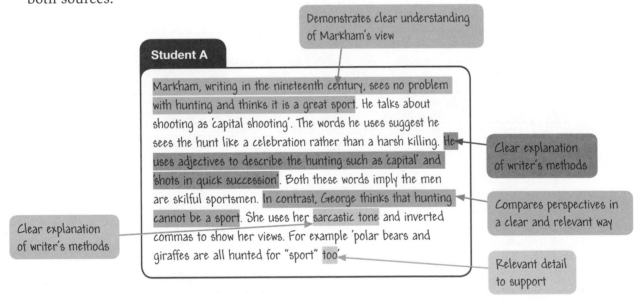

Demonstrates clear understanding of Markham's view

Student A

Markham, writing in the nineteenth century, sees no problem with hunting and thinks it is a great sport. He talks about shooting as 'capital shooting'. The words he uses suggest he sees the hunt like a celebration rather than a harsh killing. He uses adjectives to describe the hunting such as 'capital' and 'shots in quick succession'. Both these words imply the men are skilful sportsmen. In contrast, George thinks that hunting cannot be a sport. She uses her sarcastic tone and inverted commas to show her views. For example 'polar bears and giraffes are all hunted for "sport" too'.

Clear explanation of writer's methods

Compares perspectives in a clear and relevant way

Clear explanation of writer's methods

Relevant detail to support

Activity 11

Unfortunately Student A did not manage to keep up this high standard in the next paragraph. Read through the next paragraph and look at the teacher's annotations. Then rewrite it in the box below to improve it to a Grade 5 standard.

> Markham tries to make the reader share his excitement on how manly hunting is, by describing the men and the animal as strong. He makes sure that we know the tiger is strong and the words he uses make us think that everyone involved in the hunting is strong. On the other hand the other writer makes people who want to hunt as a manly thing for sport sound ridiculous and selfish.

✓

Where is a relevant supporting detail? What specific method is the writer using?

Use her name. Make it clear which text you are talking about.

Example needed from the text. Analyse specific words or phrases from the example.

Correct but now does she do this? What is her method?

20 minutes

Activity 12

Read the source texts on pages 128–130 and answer the example Question 4 below. Source A is a 2014 newspaper article by a businessman about the importance of clothes for a job interview. Source B is an advice pamphlet written by the journalist William Cobbett in 1829 about attitudes to clothing.

Example Exam Question

4 For this question, you need to refer to the *whole of Source A* together with the *whole of Source B*.

Compare how the writers have conveyed their attitudes towards clothing.

In your answer, you could:

- compare their different views and descriptions
- compare the methods they use to convey those views and descriptions
- support your ideas with quotations from both texts.

Write your answer to the question in the space below and continue on blank paper. In the exam you will be given up to four pages to write your response.

Exam tip

Remember to write about both texts. It's very easy when you are under pressure towards the end of the exam to get carried away and write about one of the texts but ignore the other.

Dress to impress: what to wear for a job interview

Don't let a fashion faux pas cost you a job. Here's how to choose the winning outfit for an interview

Tuesday 15 July 2014

The substance of your interview is, of course, key. Your patter, affability and subject knowledge are essential, but arguably your attire will also play a vital role in dictating the final outcome. First impressions are, by definition, instant and it takes seconds for a complete stranger
5 to formulate a positive or negative opinion of you based on your appearance alone.

Knowing what to wear to a job interview is an age-old conundrum. Fashions come and fashions go, but style remains, and, for both formal and informal interviews, there are a few hard and fast rules. There's no
10 room for experimentation in your interview wardrobe, so here's a guide to make sure you choose the winning outfit for the job you're applying for.

The formal interview

You should be aspiring to dress one notch above what you would normally consider suitable for work. And that of course means the job
15 that you're interviewing for. You could hang around the car park at clocking off time to get a clear indication of what people are wearing, but as a general rule of thumb, for both men and women, it's going to be a suit.

Suits never go out of fashion. There's always some rock star or hell-
20 raising actor sporting a two (or three) piece on the front page somewhere. A particular trend of the moment appears to be, what I like to call the shiny suit. These are made of a cloth that looks like it could coat a frying pan and, while it's perfectly acceptable for a wedding or a nightclub, it should not be attempted for a job interview – unless that interview
25 happens to be for a boy band.

Women

You have the choice of trousers or skirt. The rule with a skirt is that the hemline should be no more than one biro length above the knee. You can't go far wrong with black. Black is the new black after all. Navy,
30 brown and, in the summer, a lighter plain colour are also perfectly fine.

Patterns should be avoided. Add a splash of colour with a scarf, but don't get too adventurous with the shoes. Keep heels at a sensible height. Shoes can be the female equivalent of the shiny suit. Going for a plain blouse or one with a simple stripe is the safest option.

Men

35 Dark, sober colours are always good and cotton wins over linen, even in the summer – linen creases ridiculously easily. Shoes should be brown or black – black with a black, grey or blue suit, brown with a brown or blue suit. Avoid mixing black and brown and always go for leather, not suede.

40 Similarly, avoid garish patterns on ties that can distract an interviewer. Ideally the tie will complement the whole ensemble, so it should be matched with the shirt as well as the suit. It's always easiest to go with a plain, white shirt and a non-patterned, single-coloured tie. Not one that features Captain America or Homer Simpson. The same applies to your

45 socks and yes, the interviewer will notice.

Business casual

Some companies like to test your ability to interpret fashion etiquette by setting a business casual dress code. For both men and women, casual trousers and blazers can be mixed and matched, ties dispensed with and

50 even shoes can be less formal. But if it seems confusing, just follow these rules:

No jeans. No trainers. No T-shirts. Business casual – the clue's in the title.

In the final analysis, if you look great, you'll feel great and if you feel great, there will be a much higher chance of you storming your interview.

55 Whatever you decide to wear, I would recommend that you start with a fairly safe, uncomplicated canvas and add a splash, but no more, of your own personality with a well-chosen accessory.

And my own personal bug bear – make sure your shoes are polished.

Source B

Advice to young men (and incidentally young women)

by William Cobbett

Extravagance in *dress* is to be avoided. This sort of extravagance, this waste of money on the decoration of the body, **arises** solely from vanity, and from vanity of the most **contemptible** sort. It arises from the **notion**, that all the

5 people in the street, for instance, will be looking at you as soon as you walk out; and that they will, in a greater or less degree, think the better of you on account of your fine dress. Never was notion more false. All the sensible people that happen to see you, will think nothing at all about you: those who are filled with

10 the same vain notion as you are, will perceive your attempt to

---

Glossary

extravagance: wasteful, careless spending of money

arise: to come from, to originate from

contemptible: causing a person to be despised or criticised

notion: thought, idea

impose on them, and will despise you accordingly: rich people will wholly disregard you, and you will be envied and hated by those who have the same vanity that you have without the means of gratifying it.

15 Dress should be suited to your rank and station; a surgeon or physician should not dress like a carpenter! But there is no reason why a tradesman, a merchant's clerk, or clerk of any kind, or why a shopkeeper or manufacturer, or even a

20 merchant; no reason at all why any of these should dress in an *expensive* manner. It is a great mistake to suppose, that they **derive** any advantage from exterior decoration. Men are estimated by other *men* according to their capacity and willingness to be in some way or other *useful*; and though, with the foolish and vain part of *women*, fine clothes frequently

25 do something, yet the greater part of the sex are much too penetrating to draw their conclusions solely from the outside show of a man: they look deeper, and find other **criterions** whereby to judge. And, after all, if the fine clothes obtain you a wife, will they bring you, in that wife, **frugality***, good sense*,

30 and that sort of attachment that is likely to be lasting? Natural beauty of person is quite another thing: this always has, it always will and must have, some weight even with men, and great weight with women. But this does not want to be set off by expensive clothes. Female eyes are, in such cases, very

35 sharp: they can discover beauty though half hidden by beard and even by dirt and surrounded by rags: and, take this as a secret worth half a fortune to you, that women, however personally vain they may be themselves, *despise personal vanity in men*.

40 Let your dress be as cheap as may be without *shabbiness*; think more about the colour of your shirt than about the gloss or texture of your coat; be always as *clean* as your occupation will, without inconvenience, permit; but never, no, not for one moment, believe, that any human being, with

45 sense in his skull, will love or respect you on account of your fine or costly clothes.

Glossary

derive: gain
criterions: factors
frugality: to be careful with money

Progress check

Re-read your answer to Activity 12.

1. Use three different coloured pens to highlight sections of your response. Show where you have satisfied each of the criteria for a Grade 5 answer.

2. Complete the table below to assess your progress in relation to each of the Level 4 criteria.

		Yes	No
Comparing writers' ideas and perspectives	I can make simple cross-references of ideas and perspectives.		
	I can compare ideas and perspectives in a clear and relevant way.		
	I show a simple awareness of the writers' ideas and/or perspectives.		
	I show a clear understanding of the different ideas and perspectives in both texts.		
How methods are used to convey ideas and perspectives	I can make simple identification of writers' methods.		
	I can explain clearly how writers' methods are used.		
Supporting your ideas with appropriate textual references	I can make simple references to or select simple textual details from one or both texts.		
	I can select relevant detail to support from both texts.		

Overview of the Writing section

What do you need to do?

The writing section of Paper 2 is worth 40 marks, the same as the reading section. You should expect to spend about 45 minutes on your writing, with three stages to follow:

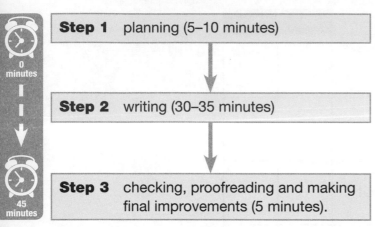

Step 1 planning (5–10 minutes)

Step 2 writing (30–35 minutes)

Step 3 checking, proofreading and making final improvements (5 minutes).

You will be given one writing task. It will be linked in a general way to the topic of the two texts read in Section A. You can draw ideas or even occasional words and phrases from the source texts if you find them useful, but you do not have to. You must not copy out complete sentences or sections.

The task will ask you to express your own views about a topic, using Standard English. You will be given a specific purpose, audience and form for your writing (for example, an article for a school magazine).

How your writing will be marked

Your writing will be marked against two Assessment Objectives:

Assessment Objective	The writing skills that you need to demonstrate
AO5 (Content and organization)	Communicate clearly, effectively and imaginatively, selecting and adapting tone, style and register for different forms, purposes and audiences.
	Organize information and ideas, using structural and grammatical features to support coherence and cohesion of texts.
AO6 (Technical accuracy)	Use a range of vocabulary and sentence structures for clarity, purpose and effect, with accurate spelling and punctuation.

The writing question in Paper 2 is worth a maximum of 40 marks:

• 20 marks are available for content and organization (AO5)

• 20 marks are available for technical accuracy (AO6).

What is content and organization?

To gain good marks for content and organization you need to:

- get your ideas across to the reader clearly
- match your writing to whatever purpose, audience and form you have been asked to write in.

You will need to make deliberate choices of language and textual features, so that your writing has the intended impact on readers. To assess this, the examiner will look at:

- the way you use individual words and phrases
- the way you sequence, link and present your points
- the organization of your whole piece of writing, and the paragraphs and sections within it.

What is technical accuracy?

Technical accuracy is using words, punctuation and grammar correctly. Your written response needs to show that you can:

- use a range of vocabulary
- spell correctly, including more complex and sophisticated words
- write in correctly punctuated sentences
- use a variety of sentence forms to achieve specific effects
- write in Standard English.

 # Progress check

Look back at your writing skills self-evaluation on pages 8–9 to remind yourself of the skills that you need to prioritize to achieve your target grade in this section.

Note down your target skills here:

The writing task

In Section B of Paper 2, the writing task is likely to present you with:

- an **assertion**, for example: 'Homework has no value'

and/or

- a statement of opinion, for example: 'Our government's push to force most young people to study traditional GCSE subjects rather than practical subjects is wrong. It ignores the range of young people in our schools and the range of skills our society needs.'

You will then be asked to write a text such as an article or letter for a particular publication, either supporting or arguing against the assertion or statement. Any audience named by the question will usually mean that you can write formally, for a general reader, rather than having to know about a specific person and their interests. This means that you must use Standard English with correct grammar, punctuation and spelling.

Look at the following example writing task.

Example Exam Question

'The youth of modern Britain are too focused on owning the latest technology or fashion and have lost the ability to enjoy the simple pleasures of life.'

Write a letter to the local MP who made this statement, in which you explain your response to her opinion.

Activity 1

Look carefully at the second part of the above writing task and identify the text type/form, audience and purpose for your writing.

Text type/form: _____

Audience: _____

Purpose: Circle the relevant terms.

to inform   to describe   to persuade   to entertain

to argue   to instruct   to explain

Key term

assertion: a confident and forceful statement of fact or belief that is presented without supporting evidence

Exam tip

When you read the writing task in the exam, the first thing you should do is identify the text type/form, audience and purpose. Use the acronym 'TAP' to help you remember this:

Text type/form: for example, a letter, speech, magazine or newspaper article

Audience: this might be the general public but could be more specific, for example, teenagers or parents

Purpose: you will be expressing your point of view, so will be writing to inform, persuade, argue or a combination of these purposes.

Planning your writing

Choosing your viewpoint

The title of Paper 2 is 'Writers' viewpoints and perspectives'. In the Writing section that writer is *you*! So you must have a **viewpoint**. Establish what you think about the topic given in the writing task before you plan and write your response.

Key term

viewpoint: the opinion of the writer on the topic in question

Activity 2

1. Look at the statements below. For each one, circle any key words that you need to consider when forming your own point of view on the topic. The first one is done for you.

2. Plot your own viewpoint in response to each statement on the line below. Remember that you will need to give reasons to support your point of view.

'The government's plans to (increase compulsory sport) in schools until students reach school-leaving age is (ridiculous.) Young people have a (right to make their own choices) about sport and fitness rather than have it forced on them in school'.

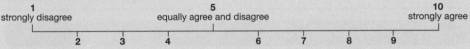

'The School Prom at 16 is a ridiculous and costly waste of time. All schools should ditch this American idea.'

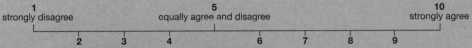

'Private schools are elitist and allow the most privileged families in society to prevent others from progressing. They should be banned in this country.'

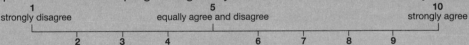

'It is time we turned off our electronic devices and actually communicated with each other face-to-face. If not, humans will lose their social skills.'

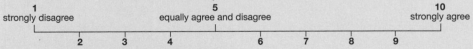

'For health and environmental reasons we should be spending more time exploring a human diet based on insects rather than animal meat.'

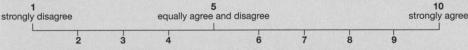

'The youth of modern Britain are materialistic. They are too focused on owning the latest technology or fashion and have lost the ability to enjoy the simple pleasures of life.'

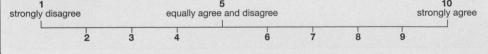

Exam tip

If the writing task in the exam presents you with a topic or issue you don't feel strongly about, you will have to adopt a viewpoint and work out some reasons to support it. 'I don't know' will not count as a viewpoint!

Identifying ideas

Once you have decided on your viewpoint, you need to identify the ideas you will present to support your point of view. You might want to use tick boxes to establish how much you agree/disagree, in your plan, for example:

1. Strongly agree – all points of argument support the statement.

2. More agree than disagree – most points of argument support the statement. A few points disagree with the statement.

3. More disagree than agree – most points of argument disagree with the statement.

4. Strongly disagree – all points of argument against the statement.

Activity 3

1. Choose the opinion above that most closely reflects your own response to the following statement:

    'The youth of modern Britain are materialistic. They are too focused on owning the latest technology or fashion and have lost the ability to enjoy the simple pleasures of life.'

2. Use this planning format to note down ideas to support your viewpoint. Outline your points to agree, disagree or a mix of both. Think carefully about any particular phrases or key words that you agree or disagree with. You could continue on blank paper.

    ☐ ☐ ☐ ☐ ☐

Student A has started to plan a response to the following writing task, circling the key words in the statement and using an opinion line:

'The (School Prom at 16) is a (ridiculous) and (costly) waste of time. All (schools should ditch) this (American idea).'

Write an article for the school newsletter in which you either agree or disagree with this view.

Student A

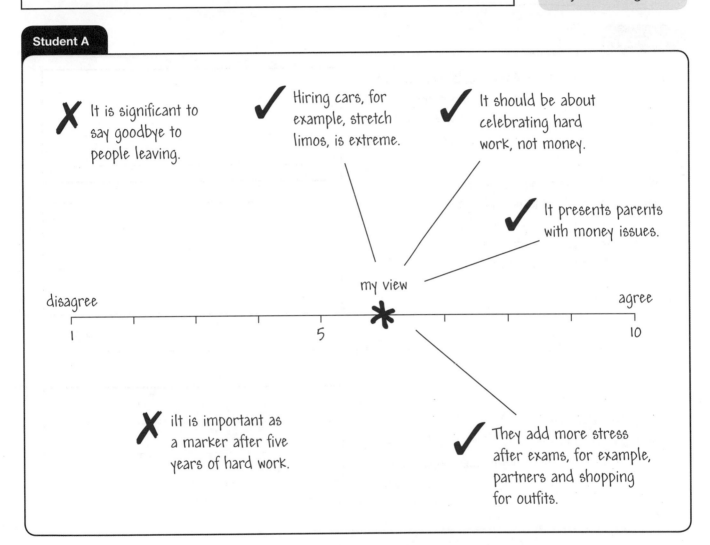

Activity 4

1. What other reasons can you think of to support the statement acknowledging the problems with school proms? Add two more clear points below:

1 _____

2 _____

Activity 4 *continued*

2. Student B completely disagrees with the statement about school proms. Look at her list of ideas below.

3. Can you identify two ideas that are very similar? Cross out one of the points that is not needed.

4. What other ideas could you add to this list to strengthen the argument? Add these to the plans.

Student B

Many people look forward to prom and it keeps them going when they are revising for exams.

Why should proms and big parties only be for adults and people that go to university? Everyone should be able to celebrate success in learning, whatever age they finish education.

my view

disagree ⁕ agree

0   5   10

Proms are not that expensive. Our prom ticket is £20 which is only the same as two cinema tickets.

Exams are tough and teenagers need a reward that they will value.

Exam tip

Beware of using the same idea or point more than once. Your argument should present and explore one idea or point per paragraph. Each idea or point must be *different* to support your view.

Structuring your writing

Once you have generated your ideas, you need to think about the way you organize these in order to create an engaging and coherent piece of writing. A helpful way to think about the structure of your writing is to decide how you want to guide your reader through your ideas to reach your conclusion. You should consider:

- how you can create an engaging opening to draw your readers in
- how you will group your ideas into paragraphs
- the most effective order in which to present your ideas
- how you can use a variety of structural features to support the **coherence and cohesion** of your writing.

Remind yourself of the example writing task.

Example Exam Question

'The youth of modern Britain are materialistic. They are too focused on owning the latest technology or fashion and have lost the ability to enjoy the simple pleasures of life.'

Write a letter to the local MP who made this statement, in which you explain your response to her opinion.

Activity 5

1. Look back at the plan you created in response to this writing task in Activity 3 and think about the following questions:

   - Is there anything you want to add or change?
   - Is each of your ideas or points different or do some overlap?
   - Have you dealt with every key aspect of the statement?
   - Have you grouped all 'agree' points together and all 'disagree' points together?
   - Have you selected the best four or five ideas to use in your plan?

2. Follow these steps to edit your plan.

   - Add any missing points.
   - Cut any repetition of ideas.
   - Ensure you have selected the best four of five ideas.
   - Number your points to decide on the best order to present your ideas.

   Use the planning formats on pages 135-137 to help you to decide on the most logical way to order your ideas. Look for connections and links between the different ideas.

   - If you are presenting a balanced viewpoint you might want to alternate points that agree and disagree with the statement or assertion.
   - If you are completely agreeing or disagreeing with the statement, you might want to build your argument and end with the strongest idea.

Exam tip

Each point or idea in your plan should provide you with a paragraph of writing. If you want to achieve a Grade 5, it is essential that you organize your writing into coherent paragraphs.

Writing your introduction

Once you have planned the structure of your writing, you need to write the introductory paragraph. The opening paragraph of your writing is important to:

- establish the topic you are considering

- set out your point of view in relation to the statement, introducing this in a general way rather than giving specific points of argument

- engage your reader and demonstrate awareness of the text type/form and purpose.

Activity 6

Three students have started to write their response to the following task.

Example Exam Question

'The School Prom at 16 is a ridiculous and costly waste of time. All schools should ditch this American idea.'

Write an article for the school newsletter in which you either agree or disagree with this view.

1. Read the opening paragraphs of their articles and decide which response you think will:

Agree with the statement ☐ Disagree with the statement ☐ Present a balanced viewpoint ☐

Student A

Satin dresses, bow ties, limos and hairspray. What more could any sixteen year old desire? Well I can certainly think of more exciting ways of spending a Friday night in July and most of them would cost half the price. School proms are definitely a stressful waste of time and I agree with you that they should be banned.

Student B

One reason that proms are a good thing is that they offer students encouragement. They know that if they get down to their revision that is going to happen soon. Lots of students look forward to them and spend a long time enjoying planning what they are going to buy, what they will wear and who they will go with.

Student C

I am writing after hearing your comment about School Proms. These are most certainly a highlight of the school year for most Year 11 students. However many teenagers, their parents and even their teachers have mixed feelings about them. They have many good points and overall I think they are a good thing, but, as you say, there are some negatives as well.

2. Annotate each introductory paragraph to identify where the student:

- establishes the topic they are considering

- sets out their point of view in relation to the statement, introducing this in a general way rather than giving specific points of argument

- engages the reader and demonstrates awareness of the text type/form and purpose.

3. Which introductory paragraph do you think is the best? Student ☐

One of the key things your introductory paragraph needs to do is engage your reader. Look at the following list of techniques you could use to do this.

Technique	Example
A rhetorical question	Why on earth have we introduced the awful American prom in this country?
A list	Satin dresses, bow ties, limos and hairspray.
A short sentence	The school prom is here to stay.
An assertion	The school prom is a ridiculous waste of time.
An interesting or shocking fact	85% of secondary schools now run a school prom to end the GCSE year.
An explanation of purpose	I am writing to you to highlight my concerns about the introduction of the school prom in the UK.
A balanced statement	The school prom may well be a waste of time for many, but for some it is the highlight of their school experience.
A short anecdote	It was only last year that my 16-year-old sister spent about three months of her life in a state of extreme anxiety; no, not about her GCSEs, but about the school prom.

Activity 7

Remind yourself of the following example writing task:

Example Exam Question

'The youth of modern Britain are materialistic. They are too focused on owning the latest technology or fashion and have lost the ability to enjoy the simple pleasures of life.'

Write a letter to the local MP who made this statement, in which you explain your response to her opinion.

1. Highlight the techniques from the table above that you would use in the introductory paragraph of a letter to your local MP.

2. Now write the opening of your letter below. Include one of the techniques listed above.

Exam tip

If you are asked to write a formal letter in the exam, remember to set out your letter in the correct format. If you know the name of the person you are writing to, sign off 'Yours Sincerely'. If you don't know the name of the person you could use 'Dear Sir or Madam' and sign off 'Yours Faithfully'.

Writing your response

When writing in the exam you must use your plan to ensure each point made is developed and supported by the sentences that follow. You should generally avoid writing a one-sentence paragraph, unless you are consciously using this structural feature for emphasis.

Activity 8

Look at the example writing task below:

Example Exam Question

'It is time we turned off our electronic devices and actually communicated with each other by sharing meals, tales and dreams. If not, humans will lose our social skills.'

Write a newspaper article in which you either agree or disagree with this view.

Student A has listed the two points he wants to include in his article:

- Computer games lead to conversation amongst friends.
- Playing computer games does not mean you eat on your own.

Now look at how the first point has been developed into a paragraph.

Student A

Computer games are not about forgetting to talk to people. If you listen to the whirlwind of conversation going on in many school playgrounds today, much of it will be about gaming. Young people share their tips and solutions so that they can get further in this virtual world. It is interesting and a way of talking. Although some people who are not interested in this world might feel left out, people who enjoy gaming talk about it a lot.

1. Write a paragraph for the second point on separate paper, adding details, evidence or an **anecdote**.

Student A

Just because you play computer games does not mean you eat on your own.

Key term

anecdote: a brief personal story, often used to add personal interest or to emphasize the writer's experience of the topic

Creating cohesion

To achieve your target grade for Section B in Paper 2, you must connect your ideas together and develop the points you make in your writing. Writing coherent paragraphs with integrated discourse markers is a key criterion for a Grade 5 response. You should not write your points as disconnected paragraphs or even as a list.

The following structures are ways to present your viewpoint and link ideas in a coherent and cohesive way. Notice that each way ends with emphasis on the point it is arguing.

Problem plus solution: Outline a problem and give a solution. The solution should be in line with the point of view you are arguing.

Cause and effect: Explain the negative or positive effects of a particular cause to support the point of view you are arguing.

Argument plus counter argument: Outline an argument that others might put forward on the topic only to dismiss that point of view with your own viewpoint.

Activity 9

Look at the following paragraphs that three students have written in response to the writing task about school proms.

1. For each paragraph, draw a line linking it to the structure it uses.

2. Circle any key words in the student response that helped you to make your decision.

| Problem plus solution | Cause and effect | Argument plus counter argument |

Student A

One negative effect of the focus on competition and money with the school prom is that parents are under pressure to spend more and more. When one teenager is taken to the prom in a Porsche, some parents feel they should better this with a stretch limo. I've even heard of people that have gone as far as a horse and cart! There seems no end to this madness!

Student B

Some people believe that the prom is an important marker of several years of hard work and is now a milestone in growing up. However, really, what is important in all this, is the grades that people leave school with that will set them up for life, rather than focusing on a party. In my opinion what marks hard work is GCSE grades; of course some of the students celebrating the prom have not really worked very hard at all, so do not really deserve a lavish party.

Student C

One major concern with the modern school prom is the fact that those that have money, dresses and enjoy this kind of event have a major celebration. But there are many students that feel very differently: they hate the idea of getting dressed up; they hate the idea of having to find a partner for the night; and they hate mainstream music and dance. The solution to this is that people should be able to join up with their own friends for their own particular celebration and not be pressurized into the major event that is the school prom.

Activity 10

Remind yourself of the following example writing task:

Example Exam Question

'The youth of modern Britain are materialistic. They are too focused on owning the latest technology or fashion and have lost the ability to enjoy the simple pleasures of life.'

Write a letter to the local MP who made this statement, in which you explain your response to her opinion.

Look back at your plan for this task and the introductory paragraph you created in Activities 3, 5 and 6. Now continue writing your letter below and complete your response on blank paper. Try to use some of the following discourse markers to connect your ideas and create coherent paragraphs:

Building your argument	Contrasting viewpoints	Asserting your point of view
It is not only the case	While some might say… others maintain	It is my view that
Similarly	Alternatively	It is undeniable that
Therefore	However	It is a well-known fact that
In relation to this	Nonetheless	It is clear to me that
As a result,	Despite this	It is generally agreed that
Not only… but also	On the other hand	
First, secondly, thirdly, finally	Conversely	
In addition	In contrast	
Another point	Unlike this	
Furthermore		
Next		

Language, tone and style

When writing your formal response in the exam, you must convey a clear tone and personal voice. Will your article add a little spark of humour? Will you adopt an indignant or sarcastic tone? Or will you adopt a serious, informed voice?

Read the text below from the end of a newspaper article by journalist Charlie Brooker. He expresses his views about how IT companies take advantage of their customers. As you read, consider the language, tone and style that Brooker has chosen in this article to describe the annoyances of modern technology.

> That little rectangular screen is so hypnotic, so omnipresent, I feel lost and sick the moment mine's tied up doing something as uninterruptable as an update. While it sits there, blank, progress bar inching along at a snail's pace, I glance at it nervously, like an owner watching his dog undergo an operation – not out of anything approaching sympathy, but the selfish concern that if it dies, I might not be able to check my email for five minutes. I suppose if I had an Apple Watch I could at least fiddle mindlessly with that instead while waiting for the phone to spring back into life. Come to think of it, that's probably the Watch's sole purpose. They should market it that way. Big winner.

Activity 11

1. Select the word below that you think best describes the tone of this article.

   impersonal   factual   impressed   furious   self-mocking

2. Select two brief quotations that you think help to create this tone and explain their effect.

   Quote 1: _____

   _____

   Effect: _____

   _____

   _____

   Quote 2: _____

   _____

   Effect: _____

   _____

   _____

Exam tip

In this article, the writer uses some informal phrases such as 'come to think of it' to engage the reader. However, the overall **style** of the article uses a formal **register** and is written in complete sentences. When writing in the exam, remember to match the register of your writing to the audience and use Standard English.

Key terms

style: the language choices a writer makes, for example, using particularly figurative language

register: the types of words and the manner of the writing, for example, formal, informal, literary; this varies according to the situation and the relationship between the reader and writer.

Look again at Brooker's article and consider the annotations that identify the language features he has used to create a skilful and engaging argument.

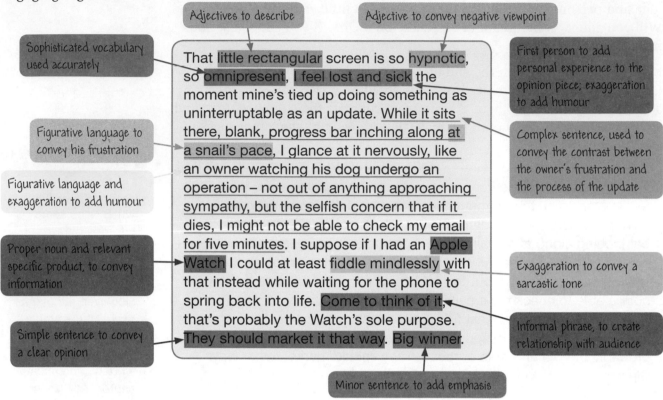

Adjectives to describe

Adjective to convey negative viewpoint

Sophisticated vocabulary used accurately

First person to add personal experience to the opinion piece; exaggeration to add humour

Figurative language to convey his frustration

Complex sentence, used to convey the contrast between the owner's frustration and the process of the update

Figurative language and exaggeration to add humour

That little rectangular screen is so hypnotic, so omnipresent, I feel lost and sick the moment mine's tied up doing something as uninterruptable as an update. While it sits there, blank, progress bar inching along at a snail's pace, I glance at it nervously, like an owner watching his dog undergo an operation – not out of anything approaching sympathy, but the selfish concern that if it dies, I might not be able to check my email for five minutes. I suppose if I had an Apple Watch I could at least fiddle mindlessly with that instead while waiting for the phone to spring back into life. Come to think of it, that's probably the Watch's sole purpose. They should market it that way. Big winner.

Proper noun and relevant specific product, to convey information

Exaggeration to convey a sarcastic tone

Simple sentence to convey a clear opinion

Informal phrase, to create relationship with audience

Minor sentence to add emphasis

Now read the following letter which responds to suggestions that the 2012 Olympics had a positive effect on people's participation in sporting activities in Britain.

The government and Sport England may well crow about the positive influence that the London Olympics had on the nation's interest in sport. Yet armchair sport is not going to make any inroads into the general health of the nation. As local authority budgets have been slashed in the last few years, facilities that used to be affordable for the majority of families are now out of the reach of many. Our local council swimming pool is expensive to maintain and prices have recently increased. A healthy trip for a family weekend swim is now less healthy for our wallets. In addition, as the price of living rises and the incomes of many fall, I know that parents are working longer and harder. There is less time for leisure and less energy amongst working adults to take their children to engage in sport.

The 'Olympic legacy' was a media construction, benefiting the few and used as a way of justifying an enormous spend of public money. Now the truth of this spend emerges, the hypocrisy of the (politically manipulated?) Olympic committee is plain to see. We are in the middle of a shocking obesity crisis. Our children are consuming higher levels of sugar resulting in tiredness and reluctance to engage in exercise. Schools are so focused on passing exams that they have little curriculum time for sport. Are the people that promoted the games really surprised that the games have had little effect on the public? Or did they know that all along? My bet is the latter.

Yours Sincerely,

Mr Smith

Activity 12

1. Select two words below which best describe the tone of the letter.

    sarcastic   amused   critical   serious

2. Now annotate the letter to identify some of the following language features. Think about how the writer uses these features to structure her writing and convey her viewpoints:

    connectives

    first-person pronoun

    personal anecdotal evidence

    points using cause and effect structure

    emotive language

    parenthesis

    statistics

    rhetorical questions

    adjectives/adjectival phrases

Activity 13

Remind yourself of the following example writing task:

Example Exam Question

'The youth of modern Britain are materialistic. They are too focused on owning the latest technology or fashion and have lost the ability to enjoy the simple pleasures of life.'

Write a letter to the local MP who made this statement, in which you explain your response to her opinion.

Look at the introductory paragraph below and continue this, using a similar tone to the one Charlie Brooker creates in the article on page 145. Think about the vocabulary choices you make and the effects these can help you create.

In fact it is not the young people of today that are materialistic and obsessed with the latest gadgets, but rather the adults. We see this all the time with the adults in our lives...

Technical accuracy

In Section B of Paper 2, you will be awarded up to 24 marks for AO5 (composition and organization) but don't forget there are 16 marks available for AO6 (technical accuracy). To ensure that you gain as many marks for AO6 as possible, make sure that you:

- re-read your writing as you go and leave enough time for a final proofread at the end
- use a wide range of punctuation accurately
- use a range of sophisticated vocabulary
- use a range of sentence forms for effect.

Using a variety of sentence forms

To achieve a Grade 5, you need to demonstrate that you can use a variety of sentence forms. Many students working below this level tend to write sentences that are all of similar length and a similar structure.

Remind yourself of the final sentences from Charlie Brooker's article:

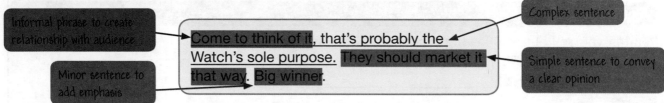

Informal phrase to create relationship with audience

Minor sentence to add emphasis

Complex sentence

Simple sentence to convey a clear opinion

Come to think of it, that's probably the Watch's sole purpose. They should market it that way. Big winner.

Notice the variety of sentence forms used. He uses short sentences for emphasis, and a longer sentence with a sub-clause to reflect his thinking aloud and reaching a conclusion.

Activity 14

Read the following extract from Student A's response:

> It is adults rather than children that are materialistic as they are the ones that are developing the products and advertising them in the first place. The queues outside the Apple Stores for new launches are full of adults and it is the young people that are passed the second-hand older models when their parents have updated to a new one. The price of these gadgets is way more than most young people can afford but actually it's more and more adults that are getting into debt and buying this kind of thing on their credit cards.

Rewrite this paragraph so that includes a variety of sentence forms. Think about how you can add vocabulary and punctuation to convey an indignant viewpoint.

Activity 15

1. Now look back at the letter you completed in Activity 10. Read through each paragraph carefully, looking for opportunities to include ambitious vocabulary, a range of linguistic devices and a variety of sentence forms to create deliberate effects.

2. Rewrite any paragraphs that you think could be improved.

Using a range of punctuation

To be able to achieve a Grade 5, you need to show that you can use a range of punctuation successfully in your writing. Remind yourself of the purpose and use of punctuation marks that might end or join sentences:

Punctuation mark	Purpose and use
Question mark ?	This could be used to ask a rhetorical question of the reader, for example, 'Where is the sense in a school prom costing over £200 per student?'
Exclamation mark !	This could be used to emphasize how ridiculous an opposing viewpoint is to you, for example, 'Some people even believe it's worth travelling to the prom in a horse and carriage!'
Ellipses …	This could be used to leave the reader thinking, for example, 'A limo. A horse and carriage. What next year's teenagers will demand we can only imagine…'
Colon :	This could be used to begin a list, for example, 'The extremes of transport choices to the Year 11 prom have become increasingly ridiculous: a horse and cart, a limo or a helicopter.'
Semi-colon ;	This should be used to link two closely connected sentences, for example, 'There seem to be no limits to what parents are expected to spend; we have seen students arrive at our prom in full-length designer evening gowns.'

Activity 16

Look back again at the letter you completed in Activity 10.

1. Could you replace full stops with any of the above punctuation marks?

2. Edit your letter to ensure you have successfully used a range of punctuation. You may need to redraft some of your sentences to enable you to do this.

Exam tip

Avoid overusing certain types of punctuation. For example, do not have a paragraph where every sentence ends with an exclamation mark or a piece of writing that is littered with questions.

45 minutes

Activity 17

Now that you have practised your writing skills, it's time to write a complete response to an example Paper 2 Section B writing task.

Example Exam Question

'There is little reason to holiday in the UK. The weather and poor facilities mean that people living in Britain should be looking further afield.'

Write an article for the travel section of a broadsheet newspaper in which you explain your point of view on this statement.

Remember to use your time carefully, dividing it between planning, writing and proofreading your work. For example:

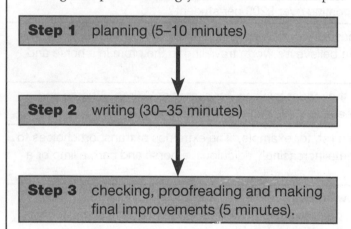

| **Step 1** | planning (5–10 minutes) |

| **Step 2** | writing (30–35 minutes) |

| **Step 3** | checking, proofreading and making final improvements (5 minutes). |

Begin your writing below and then continue on blank paper.

Progress check

Now that you have practised the skills needed to achieve a Grade 5 response to a Paper 2 Section B writing task, carry out the progress check below. Use highlighter pens of different colours to highlight passages of your answer to Activity 17 to show where you have satisfied each of the criteria for a Grade 5.

Basic skills descriptors	Check ✔	Target Grade 5 skills descriptor	Check ✔
I show a simple awareness of register and audience.		I consistently match register to audience.	
I show a simple awareness of purpose.		The content of my writing is consistently matched to purpose.	
I use simple vocabulary and some simple linguistic devices.		I use increasingly sophisticated vocabulary and phrasing for effect and use a range of linguistic devices successfully.	
I simply link one or two relevant ideas.		My writing is engaging, using a range of clear connected ideas.	
I try to use paragraphs but the structure of these is sometimes random.		I write in coherent paragraphs with integrated discourse markers.	
I use some simple structural features in my writing.		I can usually use a variety of structural features effectively	
I sometimes write in full sentences, using full stops and capital letters accurately.		I mostly write in full and accurate sentences.	
I can use some punctuation marks accurately, for example, question marks and speech marks.		I use a range of punctuation, mostly successfully.	
I use a simple range of sentence forms.		I can use a variety of sentence forms in my writing to achieve specific effects on the reader.	
I occasionally use Standard English with limited control of subject–verb agreement.		I can usually control my use of Standard English and grammar.	
I can spell basic words accurately.		I can generally spell correctly, including complex and irregular words.	
I use simple vocabulary.		I can use a range of vocabulary, including some sophisticated words.	

Sample Exam Paper 1

Source A:

This extract is from the novel Every Man For Himself *by Beryl Bainbridge, published in 1996. The novel is set in 1912 and takes place aboard the* Titanic *on her maiden voyage, which ended in disaster when the ship collided with an iceberg and sank. The novel is narrated by Morgan, a 22-year-old American man, who is on board the* Titanic *alongside fellow passengers Scurro, Hopper and Guggenheim, a wealthy American businessman. In this extract the writer describes the moment the ship began to sink.*

And now, the moment was almost upon us. The stern began to lift from the water. Guggenheim and his valet played mountaineers, going hand over hand up the rail. The hymn turned ragged; ceased altogether. The musicians scrambled upwards, the spike of the cello scraping the deck. Clinging to the rung of the ladder I tried to climb to the roof but there was such a sideways slant that I waved like a flag on a pole. I thought I must make a leap for it and   5 turned to look for Hopper. Something, some inner voice urged me to glance below and I saw Scurra again, one arm hooked through the rail to steady himself. I raised my hand in greeting – then the water, first slithering, then tumbling, gushed us apart.

As the ship staggered and tipped, a great volume of water flowed in over the submerged bows and tossed me like a cork to the roof. Hopper was there too. My fingers touched some   10 kind of bolt near the ventilation grille and I grabbed it tight. I filled my lungs with air and fixed my eyes on the blurred horizon, determined to hang on until I was sure I could float free rather than be swilled back and forth in a **maelstrom**. I wouldn't waste my strength in swimming, not yet, for I knew the ship was now my enemy and if I wasn't vigilant would drag me with her to the grave. I waited for the next slithering dip and when it came and the waves rushed in and   15 swept me higher, I released my grip and let myself be carried away, over the tangle of ropes and wires and davits, clear of the rails and out into the darkness. I heard the angry roaring of the dying ship, the deafening **cacophony** as she stood on end and all her guts tore loose. I choked on soot and cringed beneath the sparks dancing like fire-flies as the forward funnel broke and smashed the sea in two. I thought I saw Hopper's face but one eye was ripped   20 away and he gobbled like a fish on the hook. I was sucked under, as I knew I would be, down, down, and still I waited, waited until the pull slackened – then I struck out with all my strength.

I don't know how long I swam under that lidded sea – time had stopped with my breath – and just as it seemed as if my lungs would burst the blackness paled and I kicked to the surface. I had thought I was entering paradise, for I was alive and about to breathe again, and then   25 I heard the cries of souls in torment and believed myself in hell. Dear God! Those voices! *Father . . . Father . . . For the love of Christ . . . Help me, for pity's sake! . . . Where is my son.* Some called for their mothers, some on the Lord, some to die quickly, a few to be saved. The **lamentations** rang through the frosty air and touched the stars; my own mouth opened in a silent howl of grief. The cries went on and on, trembling, lingering – and God forgive me, but   30 I wanted them to end. In all that ghastly night it was the din of the dying that chilled the most. Presently, the voices grew fainter, ceased – yet still I heard them, as though the drowned called to one another in a ghostly place where none could follow. Then silence fell, and that was the worst sound of all. There was no trace of the *Titanic*. All that remained was a grey veil of vapour drifting above the water.   35

Glossary: **maelstrom:** a state of great confusion
                cacophony: a harsh mixture of loud and unpleasant sounds
                lamentations: cries or expressions of grief

Section A: Reading

Answer **all** questions in this section.

You are advised to spend about 45 minutes on this section.

---

0 1   Read the first paragraph of the source, lines 1-8.

List **four** things from this part of the text about what the narrator, Morgan, does as the ship begins to sink.

[4 marks]

A   _____

_____

B   _____

_____

C   _____

_____

D   _____

_____

0 2   Look in detail at this extract from lines 13–20 of the source:

I wouldn't waste my strength in swimming, not yet, for I knew the ship was now my enemy and if I wasn't vigilant would drag me with her to the grave. I waited for the next slithering dip and when it came and the waves rushed in and swept me higher, I released my grip and let myself be carried away, over the tangle of ropes and wires and davits, clear of the rails and out into the darkness. I heard the angry roaring of the dying ship, the deafening cacophony as she stood on end and all her guts tore loose. I choked on soot and cringed beneath the sparks dancing like fire-flies as the forward funnel broke and smashed the sea in two.

How does the writer use language to describe the narrator's experience of the ship sinking?

You could include the writer's choice of:

- words and phrases
- language features and techniques
- sentence forms.

[8 marks]

0 3   You now need to think about the **whole** of the **source**.

This text is from a key moment in the novel.

How has the writer structured the text to create a sense of drama?

You could write about:

- what the writer focuses your attention on at the beginning
- how and why the writer changes this focus as the source develops
- any other structural features that create a sense of drama.

[8 marks]

0 4   Focus this part of your answer on the second part of the source, from line 23 to the end.

A student, having read this section of the text, said: 'This part of the text shows the narrator's despair. You get a sense of the horror of the situation.'

To what extent do you agree?

In your response, you could:

- consider your own impressions of the narrator and the situation he finds himself in
- evaluate how the writer has created these impressions
- support your opinions with quotations from the text.

[20 marks]

Section B: Writing

You are advised to spend about 45 minutes on this section.

Write in full sentences.

You are reminded of the need to plan your answer.

You should leave enough time to check your work at the end

---

0 5 You have been asked to contribute to a new creative magazine for young people.

Either: write a description suggested by this picture

Or:

Write the opening part of a story in which the main character has to escape.

(24 marks for content and organization
16 marks for technical accuracy)
[40 marks]

Sample Exam Paper 2

Source A:

The Cruelest Journey by Kira Salak

Here the writer and adventurer Kira Salak describes the beginning of her 600-mile journey travelling solo in a kayak from Old Segou in Mali to Timbuktu, following the route taken along the River Niger by the 19th century explorer, Mungo Park.

Torrential rains. Waves higher than my kayak, trying to capsize me. But my boat is self-bailing and I stay afloat. The wind drives the current in reverse, tearing and ripping at the shores, sending spray into my face. I paddle madly, crashing and driving forward. I travel inch by inch, or so it seems, arm muscles smarting and rebelling against this journey.

A popping feeling now and a screech of pain. My right arm lurches from a ripped muscle.   5
But this is no time and place for such an injury, and I won't tolerate it, stuck as I am in a storm. I try to get used to the metronome-like pulses of pain as I fight the river. There is only one direction to go: forward.

I wonder what we look for when we embark on these kinds of trips. There is the pat answer that you tell the people you don't know: that you're interested in seeing a place, learning   10
about its people. But then the trip begins and the hardship comes, and hardship is more honest: it tells us that we don't have enough patience yet, nor humility, nor gratitude. And we thought that we had. Hardship brings us closer to truth, and thus is more difficult to bear, but from it alone comes compassion. And so I already discover one important reason why I'm here on this river, and I've told the world that it can do what it wants with   15
me if only, by the end, I have learned something further. A bargain, then. The journey, my teacher.

And where is the river of just this morning, with its whitecaps that would have liked to drown me, with its current flowing backwards against the wind? Gone to this: a river of smoothest glass, a placidity unbroken by wave or eddy, with islands of lush greenery   20
awaiting me like distant Xanadus.

I know there is no turning back now. The journey to Timbuktu binds me, it kidnaps and drugs me. It deceives me with images of the end, reached at long last. The late afternoon sun settles complacently over the hills to the west. Paddling becomes a sort of meditation now, a gentle trespassing over a river that slumbers. The Niger gives me its beauty almost   25
in apology for the violence of the earlier storms, and I'm treated to the peace and silence of this wide river, the sun on me, a breeze licking my toes when I lay back to rest, the current as negligible as a faint breath.

Somono fishermen, casting out their nets, puzzle over me as I float by.

"*Ça va, madame*?" they yell.   30

Each fisherman carries a young son perched in the back of his pointed canoe to do the paddling. The boys stare at me, transfixed; they have never seen such a thing. A white woman. Alone. In a red, inflatable boat. Using a two-sided paddle.

I'm an even greater novelty because Malian women don't paddle here, not ever. It is a man's job. So there is no good explanation for me, and the people want to understand.   35
They gather on the shore in front of their villages to watch me pass, the kids screaming

and jumping in excitement, the adults yelling out questions in Bambarra which by now I know to mean: "Where did you come from? Where's your husband?" And of course they will always ask: "Where are you going?"

"Timbuktu!" I yell out to the last question and paddle on.   40

Source B:

On Sledge and Horseback to Outcast Siberian Lepers by Kate Marsden

Kate Marsden was a British missionary and explorer who in 1891 set out on an expedition to Siberia to try to find a cure for leprosy. The following extract is taken from her account of this expedition which was first published in 1893. Here, she describes her journey through mosquito-infested marshes and forests.

On again for a few more miles; but I began to feel the effects of this sort of travelling – in a word, I felt utterly worn out. It was as much as I could do to hold on to the horse, and I nearly tumbled off several times in the effort. The cramp in my body and lower limbs was indescribable, and I had to discard the cushion under me, because it became soaked through and through with the rain, and rode on the broad, bare,   5
wooden saddle. What feelings of relief arose when the time of rest came, and the pitching of tents, and the brewing of tea! Often I slept quite soundly till morning, awaking to find that the mosquitoes had been hard at work in my slumbers, in spite of veil and gloves, leaving great itching lumps, that turned me sick. Once we saw two calves that had died from exhaustion from the bites of these pests, and the white hair   10
of our poor horses was generally covered with clots of blood, due partly to mosquitoes and partly to prodigious horse-flies. But those lepers – they suffered far more than I suffered, and that was the one thought, added to the strength that God supplied, that kept me from collapsing entirely...

My second thunderstorm was far worse than the first. The forest seemed on fire, and   15
the rain dashed in our faces with almost blinding force. My horse plunged and reared, flew first to one side, and then to the other, dragging me amongst bushes and trees, so that I was in danger of being caught by the branches and hurled to the ground. After this storm one of the horses, carrying stores and other things, sank into a bog nearly to its neck; and the help of all the men was required to get it out...   20

Soon after the storm we were camping and drinking tea, when I noticed that all the men were eagerly talking together and gesticulating. I asked what it all meant, and was told that a large bear was supposed to be in the neighbourhood, according to a report from a post-station close at hand. There was a general priming of firearms, except in my case, for I did not know how to use my revolver, so thought I had better   25
pass it on to someone else, lest I might shoot a man in mistake for a bear. We mounted again and went on. The usual chattering was exchanged for a dead silence, this being our first bear experience; but we grew wiser as we proceeded, and substituted noise for silence. We hurried on, as fast as possible, to get through the miles of forests and bogs. I found it best not to look about me, because, when I did so, every large stump   30
of a fallen tree took the shape of a bear. When my horse stumbled over the roots of a tree, or shied at some object unseen by me, my heart began to gallop.

Section A: Reading

Answer all questions in this section.

You are advised to spend about 45 minutes on this section.

0 1 Read again the first paragraph of Source A, lines 1–4.

Choose four statements below which are TRUE.

- Shade the boxes of the ones that you think are true
- Choose a maximum of four statements.

1	The rain is not very heavy.
2	The kayak only stays afloat due to Kira's efforts.
3	The wind helps to push the kayak forwards.
4	Kira doesn't feel as if she is making much progress.
5	Kira has to work hard to keep her kayak moving.
6	Kira suffers her injury at an inconvenient time.
7	Kira doesn't let her injury distract her.
8	The pain from her injury is constant.

[4 marks]

0 2 You need to refer to Source A and Source B for this question:

Use details from both sources. Write a summary of the similarities between Kira and Kate.

[8 marks]

0 3 You now need to refer only to Source B.

How does Marsden use language to show her feelings about her journey?

[12 marks]

0 4 For this question, you need to refer to the whole of Source A together with the whole of Source B.

Compare how the writers have described their travel adventures.

In your answer, you could:

- compare their views and experiences
- compare the methods they use to convey those views and experiences
- support your ideas with quotations from both texts.

[16 marks]

Section B: Writing

You are advised to spend about 45 minutes on this section.

You are reminded of the need to plan your answer.

You should write in full sentences.

You should leave enough time to check your work at the end.

| 0 | 5 | Children today need to take risks instead of worrying about health and safety. The school curriculum should include adventure sports and activities.

Write a letter to a national newspaper in which you argue for or against this view.

(24 marks for content and organization
16 marks for technical accuracy)
[40 marks]

Key terms glossary

anecdote: a brief personal story, often used to add personal interest or to emphasize the writer's experience of the topic

assertion: a confident and forceful statement of fact or belief that is presented without supporting evidence

coherence and cohesion: the way a piece of writing links together in terms of vocabulary, phrases, clauses, sentences and paragraphs

evaluate: to assess something and understand its quality

evidence: quotation or direct reference to the text

explanation: explanation of the effect of specific language features

explicit: stating something openly and exactly

hyperbole: a deliberately exaggerated statement that is not meant to be taken literally

implicit: not directly stated in the text, but where the meaning is suggested by the information you are given and needs to be inferred or deduced

inference: an opinion drawn from what someone implies rather than from an explicit statement

metaphor: a comparison showing the similarity between two quite different things, where one is described as the other, for example: 'the sky was a glistening fabric full of sparkle and colour'

paraphrase: express information or an idea from the source text using your own words

personification: giving human qualities or emotions to something non-human, for example, 'the flowers danced in the morning sunlight'

point: a statement that links to the question asked

register: the types of words and the manner of writing created, for example formal, informal, literary; this varies according to the situation and relationship between the reader and writer

simile: a comparison showing the similarity between two quite different things, stating that one is like the other, for example: 'his hand was like ice'

structure: the organization of a text

style: the language choices a writer makes, for example, using figurative language

synthesize: to combine information and ideas from different texts

tone: manner of expression that shows the writer's attitude, for example, a humorous, sarcastic or angry tone

viewpoint: the opinion of the writer on the topic in question